MY FAMILY KITCHEN

TOMMY PHAM

MY FAMILY KITCHEN

To Miles and Hugo, the little boys who have made me realise the importance of family. I love you and I hope that one day this book will help you to understand your Australian–Vietnamese culture.

FOREWORD — BY MELISSA LEONG

Given that my entire life revolves around food, I love to know where people stand on the subject. Not an adventurous eater? We're probably not going to bond. Can't wax lyrical about some spectacular eating experience while travelling? Ditto. Don't have a little giggle at a decent food pun? Byeeeee. It's not that I believe people who don't enjoy eating can't be delightful, it's just that if you DO love food, you tend to be the kind of person I want to be around. These legends tend to be adventurous, open minded, excited about culture, stories and, most importantly, the world around them.

Over the few short years in my role as judge on MasterChef Australia, I've definitely met people who have had an impact on my life. And in this regard, Tommy Pham has left one of the biggest. He is also, incidentally, one of the finest purveyors of food puns I have ever met. When people ask me about a dish or a cook that stands out from my time as a judge in that kitchen, it's almost always Tommy, or something that he cooked. From unapologetically funky bún mắm, to delicate bánh khọt, fish imbued with the heady aromas of dill and turmeric that is the glorious chả cá lã vọng, even his hybrid bánh mì danish, Tommy's food is full of flavour, texture and excitement.

His innate love and knowledge of Vietnamese cuisine, and just tasty food in general, is something I love and respect him for – within each dish, he offers a sense of generosity, wholehearted joy and a heaped dose of deliciousness. As a teacher and a doting dad, Tommy brings an accessible sense of fun to the kitchen; home kitchens, where kids are encouraged to watch, learn and taste, are kitchens that foster future adults with a curiosity and appreciation for food that stays with them for life.

It really takes a special person to devote their life to the wellbeing and growth of our next generations, and it fills my heart to see Tommy light up when it comes to sharing that joy he has for food, Vietnamese culture and learning in general with little humans. It requires a sense of patience as well as passion, and Tommy has both in spades.

Don't just read this book. Cook from it. Share it with the little ones in your life as a gateway to all sorts of food adventures that will incite investigation about what and why we eat what we do, and how we can learn so much about each other around the table. Because isn't that what the generosity and ritual of food is all about?

Melissa

CONTENTS

ABOUT TOMMY

WHAT UP, FAM?

My name is Tommy Pham.

I'm a former desktop engineer turned high school teacher (in Japan), turned kindergarten teacher (in Australia), turned MasterChef contestant (twice!) and now my biggest role yet – I'm a stay-at-home dad with two littlies.

I grew up in Cabramatta – better known as 'Cabra' to those who live in the area. Cabramatta is where my parents settled after fleeing Vietnam by boat before I was born in 1985. Like most immigrants, starting over in a new country with nothing meant they had to work very hard. Weekdays were for working, but weekends were for making big feasts and gathering with friends while reminiscing about the good old days . . . and singing karaoke! During these times I watched my mum create all kinds of delectable 'nhậu' foods for my dad and his friends. Nhậu is the Vietnamese word for drinking and there's no party without some yummy food to nibble. This is where my love for food began. Not knowing the difference between pig intestines and fries and nuggets, I enjoyed the food my family made and by the time I found out what some of the ingredients really were it was too late – I was already addicted! Here's a tip: feed your kids all the strange and wonderful foods before they understand what tripe really is.

As I got older my curiosity about how those foods came together led me to follow my mum into the kitchen. I remember the first recipe she taught me was for canh chua – sweet-and-sour tamarind fish soup. I was just a little too short to see what she was putting in the pot, so Mum would pull up a stool to give me a better view. First, she flavoured the soup by adding a bit of sugar, salt, fish sauce and tamarind. Mum never used any measuring spoons. Like all Asian mums she let her ancestors guide her (inside joke for those who know). Till this day canh chua is still one of my favourite dishes, maybe because of the nostalgia or maybe just because it is so damn tasty!

Being the middle child of two Vietnamese immigrant parents was not easy. As they were busy working hard to make ends meet, I became rebellious throughout my teens. Eating with Dad and cooking with Mum became secondary to skipping school and playing the video game Street Fighter.

Eventually as I got to the end of high school and into university, I stopped trying to embody the character Chan Ho Nam from the movie *Young and Dangerous* and decided to straighten up and fly right. My change in attitude (and hairstyle) led me to meet my high school sweetheart, Wendy, and that is when life really began.

A few years later we decided to move to Japan, which is when I started cooking again. What started out as necessity from missing Vietnamese food became a reignition of the flame that was lit all those years ago when Mum pulled up the little stool for me to watch her cook. I found myself calling my mum and my mum-in-law for their recipes of classic Vietnamese dishes. My repertoire was growing and so was my understanding of Asian flavours, ingredients and techniques.

My favourite thing about cooking is feeding people. Watching my friends and family enjoy my food is by far the best reward. One day when I was cooking banh xèo at a friend's house, his mum said, 'Wow, you're such a good cook. You should go on MasterChef!' And just like that, a seed was planted and off I went with my application to enter a reality TV show that would completely change my life.

Finishing in the top 10 in both MasterChef Australia series 13 and 14 was a huge accomplishment. I learnt so much about cooking, picked up heaps of skills and made lifelong friends, but nothing was as cool as the impact I had on the Asian diaspora audience watching the show. I received so many messages about how amazing it was to see authentic, traditional Vietnamese recipes on prime-time TV, to see funky ingredients used the way our families did, dishes eaten and served the right way – not the Westernised way.

After the show, I came back to my little family: Wendy – my soul mate, and my two beautiful sons Miles and Hugo. It's at home that I face the harshest judges yet. If you've got a toddler and a baby who's just started on solids, you know they are the biggest food critics of all. But luckily for me, I love them more than life itself and so it is an absolute joy to be able to cook for them as long as they will let me (even if sometimes the food ends up on the floor, or the walls, or my hair – I'm looking at you, Hugo).

INTO THE KITCHEN WITH TOMMY

Try everything once, and if you don't like it – try it again. This has always been my motto when it comes to food and it's what I hope to instil in my kids.

Growing up, I ate what my parents ate; there were no oatmeal pancakes for breakfast, no banana muffins for an after-school snack. Instead, we had chicken congee in the morning and afternoon treats were crunchy sour mangoes with chilli and salt or rice crackers dipped in fermented shrimp paste. Yum! Each dish came with a story, which meant that these delicious meals not only shaped my foodie palate but also allowed me the opportunity to immerse myself in my family's Vietnamese culture on a daily basis.

Now having children of my own, I want them to experience all of the flavours the world has to offer – from salty, sour and umami to sweet and spicy (and a little bit funky). I also want them to eat what I ate every day as a kid, with the hope that it will serve as a reminder of where their family has come from and the rich culture they're lucky to be a part of.

Once Miles was old enough to eat what we ate, I started my deep dive into Vietnamese home cooking. I found myself calling my mum and mum-in-law every night asking how to cook my favourite dishes like thit kho and canh chua. But like all true Vietnamese mums, there are no written-down recipes and no measurements for ingredients – just a little bit of fish sauce, a rice bowl of water and sugar to taste. And while having our kids eat what we eat is easy, it might not be the most nutritious for little growing bodies. I had to tweak the traditional recipes, reduce the fish sauce, hold the excessive amounts of chilli and add more vegetables. This is what led me to creating this little foodie's cookbook. I've created recipes that are based on what my

family likes to eat, but with the kiddies in mind. I've taken out the extra salt but not the flavour, replaced the unnecessary sugar with herbs and spices, and loaded vegetables wherever I could.

So, as you navigate these recipes, I encourage you to adjust the ingredients such as salt, sugar and chilli to what suits your family. Of course, I'd love for you to give my suggestions a try because it's important for flavour, but accessibility needs to champion these dishes too.

I've also tried to include bits in the recipes where kids can be involved. I love cooking with Miles and I can see that this immersion in the kitchen is already creating his love of food and a sense of exploration to try new things. Get your family together and cook up some fun and messy memories!

Inside this book you'll find lots of Vietnamese recipes from my childhood – family favourites that have been loved for generations – and also a few additions that aren't Vietnamese but have become regulars in our household and are inspired by my appreciation and love for Asian cuisine. And there are also some enjoyable activities for kids to complete in the kitchen, which is great when you spend as much time in the kitchen as I do! I hope this book sparks inspiration and motivation for your family kitchen too.

LET'S GET COOKING!

INGREDIENTS

I often get questions about what you need to start cooking Vietnamese cuisine, and there really isn't much to it. The core of Vietnamese cooking is balancing sweet, salty and sour using a few core ingredients (generally salt, sugar and fish sauce). Let's get to know some of the top ingredients used in this book.

Fish sauce – This is used in most of the savoury recipes in the book. I recommend a good quality fish sauce like Red Boat or Mega Chef, but if these aren't available, the standard Squid brand fish sauce would be my next choice.

Soy sauce – Although it isn't used widely in Vietnamese cuisine, it is still used in some of the recipes. I recommend the Lee Kum Kee brand.

Sugar – I use regular white sugar in almost all my recipes because it really helps balance out the flavours of a dish.

Salt – Although the bulk of saltiness comes from fish sauce, salt is also used to add savoury notes to a dish when the umami fish flavour isn't required. I usually use plain cooking salt.

Oyster sauce – This has a sweet and salty taste and is used in marinades or combined with other sauces such as soy or fish sauce to balance flavour. It's one of those magic sauces that makes everything taste amazing. I recommend the Lee Kum Kee Panda brand.

Herbs (coriander, mint, Vietnamese mint, shiso, Thai basil, spring onion) – These play a huge role in Vietnamese cuisine and add that quintessential freshness to a dish. If you can't find a herb to use in a recipe, I'd recommend replacing it with another similar herb. For example, if you don't have Vietnamese mint, use regular mint. The most commonly used herb in my recipes is coriander, used as a garnish, but it also adds so much more to the dish. The best place to find a wide variety of herbs is your Asian grocer. They're also often cheaper there than at the local supermarket.

Garlic – Most of my recipes use garlic, so I would suggest you make a big batch of minced garlic in a food processor and freeze it flat in a ziplock bag. When you need some, just snap off a piece and then off you go.

Noodles – The staple noodles in Vietnam are bun (rice) noodles. They come in varying sizes: from thin to thick. The thicker noodles are usually used for heartier dishes and the thinner (vermicelli) for fresher dishes. I'm partial to Vietnamese-made ones that say 'bun tuoi' on the packaging, which means fresh noodles. In my opinion they have the best texture. The wider pho noodles, used in broths and soups, are best fresh from an Asian supermarket, but of course if you can't find these, dried ones do the job as well.

Onion – This is the first ingredient in most of my soups. I always start with diced onion, sautéed in a bit of oil until soft, as the base flavour and then work from there.

Jasmine rice – Most of the dishes in this book are eaten with rice. I recommend getting a big bag of good-quality fragrant jasmine rice from your Asian grocer because it tastes way better than the rice you can get in the supermarket. When buying rice, ask for the most recent batch. I recommend the Lion brand.

EQUIPMENT

The beauty of Vietnamese cuisine is its simple cooking techniques. No need for fancy equipment – all you'll need is a few pots and pans plus some of the equipment below and you'll be cooking in no time!

Large stock pot – For the soup/broth dishes, you'll need a large pot because the ingredients, such as large veggies and bones, need space to simmer.

Muslin cloth – This is to keep spices out of broths. At a pinch, you can always use a fresh, clean Chux.

Extra-large wooden chopsticks – These can be used as your tongs, wooden spoon or spatula all in one. They're long enough to save your hands from any oil splashes and gentle enough for your non-stick pan. You can find these in a good Asian grocer.

Stock skimmer – For skimming out impurities that float to the top of broths.

Rice cooker – When you're making rice frequently, it's worth investing in a rice cooker. Sure, you can make rice in a pot on the stove, but with a rice cooker you can just set and forget.

HEY ADULTS! You'll see that most of my savoury recipes in this book have a list of optional garnishes. If you want your food to be flavoursome and pack a punch, I recommend you add these and any extra fish sauce or sugar you might like to taste for the adult portions.

MAIN MEALS

Generally speaking, Vietnamese family-style meals are a mix and match of a protein dish (món ăn mặn) and a soup dish (canh). However, the recipes in this section are complete meals or are made complete when eaten with rice (for time-sensitive parents who only want to make one dish), but if you ever feel like gaining the full Vietnamese family-style experience, make a couple of dishes (a protein, a veggie and a soup dish) and enjoy them together!

PROTEIN AND VEG

Thịt Kho

VIETNAMESE BRAISED PORK BELLY

Serves 2 adults and 2 littlies

This recipe is an all-time Vietnamese classic and I think is probably every Vietnamese child's favourite dish growing up. (It was definitely mine, that's for sure!) What's not to love about juicy, tender pork belly braised in caramelised coconut water that makes for a symphony of sweet, salty, umami goodness? Be careful though if you make this dish for your little ones, there's a high chance they will be nagging you to make it all the time!

4 large eggs

1 teaspoon vegetable oil

2 tablespoons sugar plus
    ½ teaspoon extra

1 onion, peeled and finely chopped

800 grams pork belly, cut into
    4-centimetre cubes

800 millilitres coconut water

2 tablespoons fish sauce

1 teaspoon dark soy sauce

¼ teaspoon salt

rice, to serve

To garnish

4 spring onions (shallots), rinsed,
    ends trimmed and chopped

lime wedges

2 bird's-eye chillies, chopped (parents)

Anything pickled from a jar
(I recommend Vietnamese
pickled leek or garlic)

1 Place a large pot of water over a high heat and bring to a boil. Gently add the eggs and boil for 12 minutes, then remove from the water, peel (discarding the shell) and set aside.

2 Heat the oil in a large pot over a medium–high heat and add the 2 tablespoons sugar and gently stir to evenly distribute around the pot. Cook until the sugar dissolves into a medium caramel-coloured liquid. Make sure you watch as the mixture changes colour because it can burn easily.

3 Add the onion and cook, stirring occasionally, until soft. Then add the pork belly and fry until lightly browned all over.

4 Add the coconut water and peeled eggs, and reduce to a medium heat (the liquid should just be lightly bubbling) for 30–45 minutes or until the pork is tender (the liquid should reduce by about a third). The eggs will take on the lovely caramel colour of the sauce.

5 Add the fish sauce, soy sauce, salt and the remaining ½ teaspoon sugar and stir to combine.

6 Arrange your pork belly, eggs and sauce in a serving bowl, garnish with spring onion and enjoy with rice, a squeeze of lime and offer chilli and pickles for those who are keen!

SOOOO GOOD!

Cá Hấp

SOY SAUCE STEAMED FISH

Serves 2 adults and 2 littlies

This is my everyday take on the Asian wedding banquet favourite – soy sauce steamed fish. Using fish fillets instead of a whole fish makes dinnertime so much easier and is a great way to get little ones more familiar with fish (bones terrify everyone, not only kids). I don't want to brag, but this easy dish is so good! Perfectly steamed fish combined with a sauce that brings the fish to life!

7 tablespoons vegetable oil

1 red onion, peeled and finely chopped

4 cloves garlic, minced

2 tablespoons minced lemongrass

2 teaspoons sesame oil

8 tablespoons soy sauce

2 tablespoons oyster sauce

4 tablespoons sugar

1 cup water

2 teaspoons freshly ground black pepper

2 tablespoons Chinese cooking wine or sake (optional)

750 grams white fish fillets (I love ling)

8-centimetre piece ginger, peeled and thinly sliced into matchsticks

4 spring onions (shallots), rinsed, ends trimmed and chopped (if you want to get fancy you can finely slice them lengthwise)

rice, to serve

To garnish

lime wedges

4 sprigs coriander, roughly chopped (optional)

1–2 bird's-eye chillies, sliced (parents)

1 Heat 3 tablespoons of the vegetable oil in a saucepan over a medium heat and add the onion. Fry until soft and transparent, then add the garlic and lemongrass and fry until the onion and garlic are lightly golden.

2 Add the sesame oil, soy sauce, oyster sauce, sugar, water, pepper and cooking wine (if using) and cook for 3 minutes (it doesn't need to be thick), then set aside to cool.

3 Pat the fish dry with paper towel and place on a plate that will fit inside a steamer set over a wok of simmering water. Spread the ginger on top of the fish, then gently pour half the cooled sauce over the fish (retain the rest to serve). Cover the fish with the steamer lid and increase the heat. Steam for 7–8 minutes or until the fish is a lovely, just-pull-apart texture.

4 Carefully transfer the fish from the steamer to your serving plate and sprinkle the spring onion over the top.

5 Heat the remaining oil in a pot over a high heat until it starts to smoke, then remove it from the heat and carefully pour the oil over the spring onion – listen to that sizzle!

6 Garnish your fish with a squeeze of lime and some coriander, if you like, and if you want a hit of spice, add some fresh chilli. Serve with the remaining sauce and rice.

PROTEIN AND VEG

7

Drizzle the sauce on top of rice for an extra kick of flavour!

Tommy's Tip

If you don't have a steamer, line a deep pan with baking paper and cook the fish with the sauce on low heat, covered with a lid, until just cooked!

Gà Xào Gừng

GINGER CHICKEN

Serves 2 adults and 2 littlies

This has to be one of the best bang-for-your-buck, minimal-effort-maximum-flavour dishes I know. It's crazy how fast you can whip this one up, and it will become a definite go-to when you just don't have the time but need something tasty to feed the fam!

1 tablespoon vegetable oil

4 cloves garlic, minced

4-centimetre piece ginger, finely sliced

1 kilogram free-range chicken thighs, cut into 2-centimetre chunks

⅓ cup water

1 teaspoon fish sauce

2 tablespoons oyster sauce

rice, to serve

To garnish

Squeeze of lemon or lime

2 bird's-eye chillies, chopped (parents)

2 sprigs coriander, ends trimmed and chopped

1 Heat the oil in a medium saucepan over a medium heat. Add the garlic and ginger and cook, stirring until the garlic softens.

2 Add the chicken, then turn the heat up to high and sear the meat, turning, until it has lightly browned all over.

3 Add the water, fish sauce and oyster sauce, stirring until evenly distributed, then cook on medium heat for 15 minutes or until the sauce has just thickened.

4 Serve the chicken over rice and garnish with a squeeze of lemon, chilli (for parents, if using) and some coriander.

Japanese Miso Salmon

Serves 2 adults and 2 littlies

This dish is one of my favourite recipes, and I discovered it when I was living in Japan. Although it isn't Vietnamese, it's a dish I always come back to when I am out of meal ideas, so I had to share! Miles always enjoys this dish because he gets a chance to make his own sushi rolls. We usually serve the fish with a side of cucumber sticks, Japanese pickles, sheets of nori, Japanese mayonnaise and rice.

6 tablespoons white miso

4 tablespoons sugar

4 tablespoons mirin

2 tablespoons sake (optional)

1 packet dashi powder

800 grams salmon fillets, cut in 4-centimetre pieces

3 spring onions (shallots), rinsed, ends trimmed and chopped

1 avocado, halved and sliced

1 cucumber, cut into 4-centimetre sticks

Japanese pickles (optional)

1 packet nori seaweed, sheets cut into quarters

rice, to serve

Condiments

Kewpie mayonnaise

soy sauce

wasabi (parents)

shichimi (parents)

1 Mix the miso, sugar, mirin, sake (if using) and dashi together in a large bowl until smooth.

2 Place the salmon pieces into the marinade and gently mix to cover.

3 Cover the salmon and marinate in the fridge for 6–48 hours.

4 Remove the salmon from the marinade. Gently scrape as much of the marinade off as you can – I usually use a spoon for this.

5 Place the salmon on a baking tray lined with baking paper, skin-side down.

6 Heat the oven grill to 180°C.

7 Place the salmon fillets on the middle rack of the oven. Grill for 6 minutes, then flip and cook for another 90 seconds.

8 Remove the salmon from the grill and rest for 5 minutes.

9 Garnish the salmon with spring onion and enjoy with the veggies, nori and rice. Offer mayo, soy sauce, wasabi and shichimi separately.

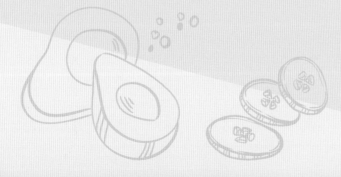

Su Su Xào Trứng

STIR-FRIED CHOKO AND EGG

Serves 2 adults and 2 littlies

This is a very basic stir-fry recipe that takes almost no time to prepare. If you have ever seen the oddly shaped green vegetable, choko, and wondered how to use it, here's your chance! It's a great flavour absorber and has a nice crunch to it. I'll be honest, I love to pair this with some good old sliced and pan-fried spam. It's my little secret!

2 teaspoons vegetable oil

½ brown onion, peeled and diced

5 cloves garlic, minced

3 chokos, peeled and cut into matchsticks

1 tablespoon water

2½ teaspoons fish sauce

½ teaspoon salt

½ teaspoon sugar

4 large eggs

¼ teaspoon soy sauce

cracked black pepper (optional)

rice, to serve

1 Heat the oil in a large saucepan over medium heat, then add the onion and fry for 2 minutes or until fragrant and soft.

2 Add the garlic and fry until fragrant and soft.

3 Add the choko and water and cook for 5 minutes or until the choko is just soft.

4 Add 1½ teaspoons of the fish sauce, ¼ teaspoon of the salt and ¼ teaspoon of the sugar, then stir and fry until evenly mixed.

5 Beat the eggs in a small bowl with ½ teaspoon of the fish sauce and the remaining ¼ teaspoon sugar.

6 Turn the heat to medium–high and slowly pour the egg mixture in to cover the choko.

7 Gently stir until the egg is just cooked.

8 Add the remaining ½ teaspoon fish sauce, the soy sauce and the remaining ¼ teaspoon of salt and gently stir to combine.

9 Finish with cracked black pepper, if using, and serve with steamed rice.

Easy Fried Rice

Serves 2 adults and 2 littlies

Everyone loves fried rice, especially kids. Maybe because it's colourful and easy to scoop up with a spoon. I know we love fried rice in our household because it's quick to make and you can add lots of veggies. This recipe uses frozen veggies and eggs, which makes it perfect for when you don't feel like hitting the shops to buy ingredients. Like most fried rice, it comes out better when you use day-old leftover rice because it's drier and the grains fall apart more easily when you fry it.

3 cups frozen peas, corn and carrots

water

1½ tablespoons vegetable oil,
   plus 2 teaspoons extra

5 cloves garlic, minced

3 cups day-old, cooked rice

1½ tablespoons soy sauce

1 teaspoon fish sauce

¼ teaspoon salt

¼ teaspoon white sugar

2 teaspoons sesame oil

4 eggs, lightly whisked

3 spring onions (shallots), rinsed,
   ends trimmed and chopped

To garnish

chilli oil (parents)

sriracha (parents)

1 Place the peas, corn and carrots in a large microwave-safe bowl, add a splash of water, cover with a plate and microwave for 3 minutes. Drain, then set the vegetables aside.

2 Place 1½ tablespoons of the vegetable oil in a hot wok or large frying pan over a high heat until the oil just starts to smoke. Add the garlic and fry for 1 minute, then add the cooked peas, corn and carrots and cook for 2 minutes.

3 Add the rice and stir through, then add the soy sauce, fish sauce, salt, sugar and sesame oil and stir again, cooking until the sauce evaporates.

4 With a spatula or large spoon, push the rice to the edges of the wok/pan to make a large well in the centre, then add the remaining 2 teaspoons of vegetable oil in the centre and heat for 1 minute.

5 Add the whisked eggs and cook for 3–4 minutes or until the egg has cooked through. Then add the spring onion and mix well until you have the perfect fried rice.

6 To garnish, combine a little chilli oil and sriracha and sprinkle over the top.

Tommy's Tip

If you don't have day-old rice, you can spread your rice on a sheet pan and place it in the fridge, uncovered, for as long as you can to dry it!

Leftovers are great for lunchboxes and will have all the other kids drooling over your little one's lunch!

Cà Tím Nướng Mỡ Hành

GRILLED EGGPLANT WITH SPRING ONION OIL

Serves 2 adults and 2 littlies

Top soft, creamy, perfectly cooked eggplant with a fatty spring onion oil and a sweet–salty–sour nước mắm dressing and you've got yourself a dish that will please everyone!

3 large (or 4 medium) eggplants

5 tablespoons vegetable oil

3 spring onions (shallots), rinsed, ends trimmed and roughly chopped (makes approximately ¾ cup)

¼ teaspoon salt

¼ teaspoon sugar

rice, to serve

Nước mắm dressing

4 tablespoons fish sauce

4 tablespoons sugar

6 tablespoons warm water

2½ tablespoons lime juice or rice wine vinegar

2 cloves garlic, minced

1–2 bird's-eye chillies, minced (parents)

To garnish

⅓ cup roasted peanuts, crushed

1 Poke the eggplants with a skewer about 10 times evenly around the eggplant, then either air fry at 200°C for 20–25 minutes or bake in an oven at 180°C for 45 minutes. Either way, the eggplants should be cooked all the way through.

2 To make the nước mắm dressing, combine the fish sauce, sugar, water, lime juice or rice wine vinegar, garlic and chilli (if using) in a bowl and mix until the sugar has dissolved. Set aside.

3 Heat the oil in a small saucepan over high heat until hot (to test, add a slice of spring onion – if it bubbles up, the oil is ready), then add the spring onion, salt and sugar and cook for 30 seconds or until the spring onion is just soft.

4 Peel the eggplants, keeping the stems on to keep the flesh together, then place the eggplants on a large plate. Drizzle some nước mắm dressing over the eggplant, and serve the remaining dressing in a dish. Then spoon the spring onion oil over and garnish with roasted peanuts. Serve with rice.

Tommy's Tip

To save time I use an air fryer to cook the eggplants instead of baking them in the oven: This cuts the cooking time in half. Honestly, if you are raising a family and don't have an air fryer, take this as a sign! Air fryers are a must for families on the go!

Serve as a light dinner
or filling lunch.

Chả Trứng Chiên

VIETNAMESE EGG OMELETTE

Serves 2 adults and 2 littlies

This is your basic egg and rice dish, but taken to the next level. The pork mince mixed with egg makes for a filling protein option that is a bit heartier than regular fried egg!

1 tablespoon dried shredded wood-ear mushroom soaked for 20 minutes then drained

5 large eggs, beaten

½ brown onion, peeled and diced

1 spring onion (shallot), rinsed, ends trimmed and chopped

200 grams pork mince

3 teaspoons fish sauce

½ teaspoon soy sauce

¼ teaspoon salt

¼ teaspoon sugar

1 teaspoon vegetable oil

rice, to serve

To garnish

2 Lebanese cucumbers, sliced

1 Place the dried wood-ear mushroom in a small bowl and add enough boiling water to cover it.

2 In a large bowl, place the eggs, brown onion, spring onion, pork, fish sauce, soy sauce, salt and sugar, then mix with a spatula until blended.

3 Heat the oil in a large non-stick pan over high heat until hot. Turn the heat down to medium, add the egg and pork mixture and spread to even out the omelette.

4 Cook for 3–4 minutes or until the omelette is about halfway cooked through. Be careful here and make sure you check the bottom of the omelette to make sure it doesn't burn.

5 Flip the omelette and cook for another 2–3 minutes until the bottom is golden. This step is no easy task, so it's good to know that the more cooked through the omelette, the easier it will be to flip.

6 Remove the omelette from the pan and place on a large plate. Serve with rice and cucumber on the side.

Tommy's Tip
Make a quick nước mắm dressing (see page 15) if you'd like something to drizzle over the dish to give it an extra kick of flavour!

SOUPS

Bún Thang

HANOI CHICKEN NOODLE SOUP

Serves 2 adults and 4 littlies

Every culture has its own version of chicken noodle soup and this one originated from Hanoi, Vietnam. This dish is less of a flavour hit and more of a healing, simple broth, which is great for when you feel a bit under the weather and just crave something to nurture your insides. Kids will love the colour of the vegetables cut up into bite-sized strips to entice even the pickiest eaters.

1 free-range whole chicken (about 1.5 kilograms)

4 tablespoons dried shrimp, chopped

3-centimetre piece ginger, halved lengthways

2 brown onions, halved

1 carrot, quartered

2 litres water

1 packet rice vermicelli noodles

1¼ teaspoons vegetable oil

200 grams king oyster mushrooms, washed and thinly sliced

¾ teaspoon salt

½ teaspoon sugar

3 large free-range eggs

1½ tablespoons fish sauce

2 teaspoons chicken bouillon powder or bone broth powder (optional)

To garnish

5 spring onions (shallots), rinsed, ends trimmed and chopped

5 sprigs coriander, ends trimmed and chopped

1 bunch Vietnamese mint, washed and leaves chopped

1 packet fried shallots

1 red onion, peeled and finely sliced

lime wedges

bird's-eye chilli, sliced (parents)

cracked black pepper (parents)

¼ teaspoon mam tom or fermented shrimp paste (parents)

soy sauce (optional)

See over the page for the cooking steps.

1 Place the chicken, dried shrimp, ginger, onion, carrot and water into a large pot and bring to a boil.

2 Turn down heat to medium–low and simmer for approximately 25 minutes. Use a large, flat spoon to skim off any 'nasties' at intervals.

3 Remove the whole chicken from the pot and cover it with cling wrap. Let it cool in the fridge for 10 minutes before shredding the flesh with a fork.

4 Place a lid back on the pot and cook the broth on a low heat while you prep the other ingredients – it should barely bubble.

5 In a separate pot, cook the noodles according to the packet instructions. Strain, rinse with cold water and set aside.

6 Heat 1 teaspoon of the vegetable oil in a non-stick pan on high heat, adding the king oyster mushrooms and fry until soft. Add ¼ teaspoon of the salt and ¼ teaspoon of the sugar to season. Remove from the heat and set aside for later.

7 In a small bowl, beat the eggs, ½ teaspoon of the fish sauce and the remaining ¼ teaspoon sugar in a small bowl until well combined.

8 Heat a little oil in a non-stick pan on medium heat. Pour some of the egg mixture into the pan so there's just enough of the mixture covering the pan (think crepes but a little thicker). Cook until the egg starts to look opaque (about 15 seconds), then flip and cook for another 5 seconds.

9 Transfer the sheet of egg to a plate and repeat with the remaining egg mixture, stacking the egg sheets as they are ready.

10 Roll the stack of egg sheets, then cut into thin strips and set aside for later.

11 Add the chicken bouillon powder (optional), remaining 1 tablespoon fish sauce, ½ teaspoon salt and ¼ teaspoon sugar to the chicken broth.

12 Remove the ginger and onion from the broth with a slotted spoon.

13 To serve, place a handful of rice noodles in each bowl. Top with shredded chicken, egg and king oyster mushrooms. Pour over the broth.

14 Add garnishes and enjoy.

Canh Cà Chua Trứng

TOMATO, PORK AND EGG SOUP

Serves 2 adults and 2 littlies

This recipe is an everyday lazy dish that is super flavourful, homey and just so easy to eat. I honestly think it's the simple flavours that make you feel like coming back for more. I usually have most of the ingredients for this dish at home, because when you think about it, all you really need is some pork mince and tomatoes – the rest of the ingredients are pretty much pantry staples (well, at least to me, ha ha). This is the reason I whip up this dish whenever I can't think what I want to feed the family. It's quick, tasty and no fuss!

2 teaspoons vegetable oil

1 brown onion, finely chopped

400 grams pork mince

6 vine-ripened tomatoes, cut into small wedges

1 teaspoon fish sauce plus 1 tablespoon extra

½ teaspoon salt

½ teaspoon sugar

1 litre water

6 large eggs, lightly beaten

rice, to serve

To garnish

4 spring onions (shallots), rinsed, ends trimmed and chopped

4 sprigs coriander, ends trimmed and chopped

2 bird's-eye chillies, chopped (parents)

1 Heat 1 teaspoon of the oil in a large pot over a medium heat, then add the onion and fry until soft and fragrant.

2 Increase the heat to medium–high, then add the pork and fry until it is lightly browned all over.

3 Add the tomato and cook, stirring, for 8 minutes or until the tomato is soft and forms a loose paste.

4 Add 1 teaspoon of the fish sauce, salt and sugar and fry for 30 seconds.

5 Pour the water into the pot and bring to the boil, add the remaining 1 tablespoon of fish sauce, then reduce to medium–low and simmer for 5 minutes to cook the tomato.

6 Slowly pour the egg into the soup while gently stirring.

7 Garnish with spring onion and coriander, and chilli if you like, and serve with rice.

Canh Xương Heo Khoai Tây Cà Rốt

PORK SPARE RIB SOUP WITH POTATO, CARROT AND BEANS

Serves 2 adults and 2 littlies

This is a one-pot wonder. Perfect for when it's cold out or you're feeling under the weather. The best thing about this dish is that it uses inexpensive ingredients that are easily accessible. Chop 'em up and chuck 'em in a big old pot and dinner will be ready in no time. Enjoy this with a side of steaming hot rice or just on its own.

2 teaspoons vegetable oil

2 large potatoes, peeled
and cut into large chunks

1.2 kilograms pork spare ribs (soft bone),
cut into 3-centimetre pieces

2 carrots, peeled and cut into
3-centimetre chunks

1 brown onion, peeled and halved

1.5 litres water

1 tablespoon fish sauce

1 teaspoon salt

¼ teaspoon sugar

1 x 400 gram can cannellini beans,
drained and rinsed

To garnish

2 spring onions (shallots), rinsed,
ends trimmed and chopped

2 sprigs coriander, ends trimmed
and chopped

2–3 bird's-eye chillies (optional),
finely sliced

lime wedges

fish sauce

1 Add the oil to a large pot on high heat, then put in the potato and cook for 5 minutes while constantly flipping until the edges are sealed and slightly golden. Add the pork and cook for 4 minutes until the meat has just sealed and is golden.

2 Add the carrot, onion and water to the pot and bring to a boil. Then turn down the heat to medium and simmer for approximately 20 minutes or until the meat and potato are tender. Skim the surface scum or residue from the top of the soup while it is simmering.

3 Add the fish sauce, salt, sugar and beans to the pot and stir. Cook until the beans have warmed through.

4 To serve, garnish with spring onion and coriander. Parents add chilli, lime and a dash of fish sauce into their bowls if desired.

Canh Cà Tím Đậu Hũ

TURMERIC PORK, EGGPLANT AND FRIED TOFU SOUP

Serves 2 adults and 2 littlies

This is a Northern Vietnamese dish that I have recently become obsessed with because it has a stronger flavour hit than other soups as it uses a bit of turmeric and a lot of garlic. If you've got the time, hit up the Asian grocer for this one as you'll need fried tofu, shiso and turmeric. This is also a great recipe to get eggplant and tofu on the menu.

2 tablespoons vegetable oil

½ brown onion, peeled and diced

800 grams pork belly, thinly sliced then cut in 3-centimetre pieces

1 small Lebanese eggplant, quartered and cut into wedges

1½ tablespoons fish sauce

½ teaspoon sugar

2 tomatoes, cut into small wedges

1 pack fried tofu puffs (approximately 280 grams)

1.4 litres water

½ teaspoon ground turmeric

1 teaspoon salt

3 cloves garlic, minced

rice, to serve

To garnish

2 spring onions (shallots), rinsed, ends trimmed and chopped

2 sprigs coriander, ends trimmed and chopped

½ bunch shiso, roughly chopped

2–3 bird's-eye chillies, finely sliced (parents)

1 Place the oil in a large pot on high heat. Add the onion and cook until it is soft, then add the pork and cook for 4 minutes or until there is a slightly golden seal on the meat. Add the eggplant and mix in 1 teaspoon of the fish sauce and ¼ teaspoon of the sugar.

2 Add the tomato, tofu, water, turmeric, salt and the remaining fish sauce and sugar and bring the pot back to a boil.

3 Turn the heat down to medium and simmer until the eggplant is soft, approximately 10 minutes.

4 Add the garlic and simmer for 2 minutes to soften.

5 To serve, garnish with spring onion, coriander, shiso and chilli (if using). Enjoy with rice.

Canh Thịt Bò Cà Chua

BEEF, TOMATO AND GAI LAN SOUP

Serves 2 adults and 2 littlies

You know the leafy greens that you get at yum cha? They're called gai lan (Chinese broccoli) and that is what you'll need to make this tasty soup. This is a great way to introduce the littlies to this Asian veggie staple because the base flavours are familiar – tomato and beef.

1 teaspoon vegetable oil

6 cloves garlic, minced

4 vine-ripened tomatoes, cut into small wedges

1 tablespoon fish sauce

½ teaspoon sugar

½ teaspoon salt

1 litre water

2 bunches gai lan (Chinese broccoli), roughly chopped and bruised

600 grams beef rump, finely sliced

rice, to serve

To garnish

3 spring onions (shallots), rinsed, ends trimmed and chopped

3 sprigs coriander, ends trimmed and chopped

2 bird's-eye chillies, chopped (parents)

1 Heat the oil in a large pot on medium heat. Add the garlic and fry until soft and fragrant.

2 Add the tomato, ½ teaspoon of the fish sauce, ¼ teaspoon of the sugar and ¼ teaspoon of the salt and cook until the tomato just softens.

3 Add the water and bring to a boil.

4 Add the gai lan and cook for 3–5 minutes on medium or until the gai lan is just cooked but still has a bite to it.

5 Add the beef and poach until it is just cooked through.

6 Garnish with spring onion, coriander and chilli (if using), then enjoy with rice.

Tommy's Tip

To make sure that the gai lan absorbs the flavour, cut the stems at an angle and then bruise the leaves by rubbing them against each other in your hands.

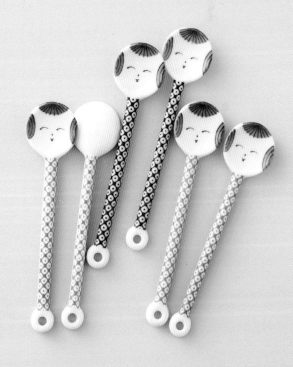

Canh Bí Đỏ Thịt Bằm

VIETNAMESE PUMPKIN AND PORK SOUP

Serves 2 adults and 2 littlies

This recipe is a great one to keep up your sleeve because it's super simple and packed with the good stuff. You've probably got most of the ingredients at home right now – just grab some pumpkin and pork mince and you're good to go! When I say pumpkin soup, most people would think of a thick soup, but this is completely different! This is a super-clean pork broth with poached pumpkin that you serve with rice on the side. The savoury broth pairs perfectly with the sweet pumpkin! This dish is one that my little boy Miles has absolutely loved since he first started eating proper food. It's great for winter or for when the little ones are feeling a little sniffly.

1½ teaspoons vegetable oil

½ brown onion, peeled and finely chopped

250 grams pork mince

3 teaspoons fish sauce

¼ teaspoon salt

800 grams Kent pumpkin, skin removed and roughly chopped

3 cups water

rice, to serve

To garnish

3 spring onions (shallots), rinsed, ends trimmed and finely chopped

1 bird's-eye chilli, chopped (parents)

cracked black pepper

1 Place the oil and onion in a pot over a medium heat, and cook until soft.

2 Add the pork mince and fry, stirring to break up the meat, for 5 minutes or until the meat is lightly browned all over.

3 Add ½ teaspoon of the fish sauce and the salt, pumpkin and water to the pot and bring to a boil, then place the lid slightly askew and simmer for 10–15 minutes or until the pumpkin is soft.

4 Add the remaining fish sauce to the pot.

5 Serve the soup garnished with some spring onion, chilli, if using, and pepper, and enjoy with rice.

Perfect for a cold day!

Súp Măng Cua

ASPARAGUS AND CRAB SOUP

Serves 2 adults and 2 littlies

This soup is perfect for those colder spring days when you need a little bit of warmth. What's even better is that you only need five ingredients (minus pantry ingredients) and five steps! Yes, I use canned crab in the recipe, but that's because this is usually a spur-of-the-moment kind of dish for me. I would usually have all the other ingredients at home and would rather not run out to go grab some crab! This is why I specify a good quality can of crab meat. To me, what makes this dish is the garnishes and toppings. Don't get me wrong, the soup is great, but the garnishes really give the soup a pop of flavour!

2 bunches asparagus, hard ends removed and roughly chopped

2 litres salt-reduced chicken stock

1 x 140 grams can crab meat (the good expensive stuff!)

2 eggs, beaten

¼ cup potato starch

½ cup cold tap water

salt, to season

sugar, to season

To garnish

drizzle of black vinegar

3–4 spring onions (shallots), rinsed, ends trimmed and chopped

½ bunch coriander, ends trimmed and chopped

cracked black pepper, to taste

sesame oil, to taste

1 Add the asparagus and stock to a pot and place over a high heat. Bring to a boil and cook for 5 minutes or until the asparagus is tender.

2 Add the crab meat (including its juices) and bring to a boil.

3 Place a sieve over the pot and pour the beaten eggs through the sieve into the soup and mix thoroughly. This process allows the egg to drizzle into the soup and gives a lovely silky texture.

4 In a bowl, mix the potato starch and water until smooth (this makes a 'slurry'), then slowly pour the slurry into the pot while mixing.

5 Season with a pinch of salt and sugar, add optional toppings and enjoy!

Canh Mướp

PRAWN AND LUFFA SOUP

Serves 2 adults and 2 littlies

Luffa is a type of gourd (or hard-shelled vegetable) and funnily enough it's the same vegetable that makes a shower loofah. Luckily, the luffas in this recipe are a lot softer and more edible than the ones you wash yourself with! You can find luffas in most Asian supermarkets and they have a very interesting texture compared to your average vegetable. Soft and a little bit spongy, luffas cook almost instantly and absorb a lot of flavour from the broth. Make sure you don't overcook them or you'll lose that amazing texture.

3 tablespoons dried shrimp

2 tablespoons boiling water

¼ teaspoon vegetable oil

1 brown onion, peeled and diced

10 large prawns, peeled, deveined and cut into 1-centimetre pieces

3 teaspoons fish sauce

½ teaspoon salt

½ teaspoon sugar

3½ cups water

1 large luffa gourd (or 2 medium-sized ones), peeled and cut into 2-centimetre pieces

rice, to serve

To garnish

4 spring onions (shallots), rinsed, ends trimmed and chopped

cracked black pepper (optional)

2 bird's-eye chillies, chopped (optional)

1 Place the dried shrimp in a small bowl and pour over the boiling water. Soak for 10 minutes.

2 Remove the dried shrimp from the liquid, reserving the liquid for later. Mince the shrimp as finely as possible by chopping and mashing them with a knife on a chopping board or in a food processor to make a paste. Set aside.

3 Heat the oil in a large pot on medium heat. Add the onion and cook for 2 minutes or until soft.

4 Add the shrimp paste and the prawns, and ½ teaspoon of the fish sauce, ¼ teaspoon of the salt and ¼ teaspoon of the sugar to the pot and cook for 2 minutes or until fragrant.

5 Add the liquid you soaked the shrimp in to the pot, along with the water and the luffa gourd, then turn the heat to high and bring to a boil.

6 Turn the heat down to medium and simmer for approximately 2 minutes or until the luffa gourd is just soft.

7 Add the remaining seasonings (fish sauce, salt and sugar) to the pot.

8 Remove from the stove, place in a bowl and top with garnishes. Serve with rice.

Canh Bí Đao

HAIRY MELON WITH PORK SOFT BONE RIBS

Serves 2 adults and 2 littlies

Hairy melon has a very interesting texture. If I had to compare it to other vegetables in this book, it would be in between a luffa and a kohlrabi, soft but with a tiny bit of bite! Kids love gnawing at the ribs in this soup so that will give you some bonus quiet time at the dinner table. Combine this with some rice and you've got a soulful, healing meal!

1 teaspoon vegetable oil

½ brown onion, peeled and finely chopped

1 kilogram pork spare ribs (soft bone), cut into 3-centimetre pieces

1.4 litres water

1 hairy melon, peeled, halved, deseeded and cut into 3-centimetre chunks

2½ teaspoons fish sauce

¼ teaspoon salt

¼ teaspoon sugar

To garnish

2 spring onions (shallots), rinsed, ends trimmed and chopped

2 sprigs coriander, ends trimmed and chopped

1 bird's-eye chilli, chopped (parents)

lime wedges

fish sauce

1 Place the oil in a large pot over a high heat, then add the onion and cook for 2 minutes or until soft.

2 Add the pork and cook for 4 minutes or until the meat is lightly sealed and golden.

3 Add the water and bring to a boil, then reduce the heat to medium and simmer for 15 minutes or until the meat is tender.

4 Use a large, flat spoon to skim off any nasties from the top of the soup.

5 Add the hairy melon, then bring the mixture back to a boil. Reduce the heat back to medium and simmer for 2–3 minutes or until the melon is just cooked through and slightly transparent.

6 Add the fish sauce, salt and sugar and stir to combine.

7 Serve the soup in bowls and garnish with spring onion and coriander. If you fancy more spice, add some chilli, a squeeze of lime and a dash of fish sauce.

Canh Chua Cá

SWEET-AND-SOUR SOUP WITH FISH

Serves 2 adults and 2 littlies

This dish is a wonderful assault on the senses. The sweetness from the pineapple, the sourness from the tamarind and the savoury-ness from the fish makes the perfect harmony of flavours! I use canned pineapple in juice here just because I like to save time when cooking in the kitchen for my family, but feel free to use fresh pineapple. There are many variations of this dish, and this one is my basic version. Think of it as the minimum you need to make this dish, but feel free to add other vegetables such as okra, elephant ear stalks (not from elephants ha ha), bean sprouts or enoki mushrooms. You can also swap the fish out for chicken wings (my mum's favourite version) or silken tofu if you want to go vego!

1½ tablespoons vegetable oil

4 cloves garlic, minced

1 litre water

3 large ripe truss tomatoes,
   cut into wedges

4 slices pineapple from a can (or 250 grams
   fresh pineapple), cut into chunks

5 teaspoons tamarind puree

1½ tablespoons fish sauce

1–1½ tablespoons sugar

¼ teaspoon salt

3 teaspoons pineapple juice reserved from
   can (add 1 teaspoon sugar if you use fresh
   pineapple)

500 grams barramundi fillets, cut into
   3-centimetre pieces

200 grams beans sprouts, plus extra
   for crunch

rice, to serve

To garnish

crispy garlic oil (prepared above)

½ bunch rice-paddy herb or Thai basil,
   chopped

2–3 bird's-eye chillies, sliced (parents)

bean sprouts

1 To make crispy garlic oil, add the oil and garlic to a small pan over a medium heat. Fry until the garlic is lightly coloured, then pour the mixture into a small bowl and set aside.

2 Place the water, tomato, pineapple and tamarind puree in a pot over a high heat and bring to a boil.

3 Reduce the heat to medium and simmer for 6–8 minutes or until the tomato starts to soften and break down.

4 Add the fish sauce, 1 tablespoon of the sugar, the salt and the reserved pineapple juice to the broth and stir to combine.

5 Add the fish and bean sprouts to the pot and cook on a gentle simmer for 4 minutes or until fish is just cooked through. Taste the broth – it should be a nice balance of sweet, salty and sour. Add 1 teaspoon of the remaining sugar and taste: if it's not sweet enough, add the final teaspoon. (You can always add a bit more if you like it even sweeter.)

6 Transfer to a large serving bowl or individual bowls, then garnish with the crispy garlic oil, herbs and bird's-eye chilli. If you like some extra crunch, top with extra bean sprouts, and serve with rice.

The classic garnish for this dish is rice-paddy herb, which is a super-fragrant herb. It does wonders and you can usually find it at Vietnamese grocers, but if you're having trouble finding it you can always replace it with Thai basil, as I have here.

Canh Su Hào

CHICKEN AND KOHLRABI SOUP

Serves 2 adults and 2 littlies

Kohlrabi is the funny-looking veggie that you may have seen recently in the supermarket. Previously I could only find it at Asian grocers, but nowadays it's becoming mainstream and I can definitely see why. It's super clean tasting and sweet – the perfect addition to any basic soup as the natural sweetness means you don't have to add much sugar (always a win when cooking for the littlies). Just like the choko, kohlrabi also absorbs flavours very well.

½ teaspoon vegetable oil

1 brown onion, peeled and diced

4 chicken thighs, cut into bite-sized pieces

2 kohlrabies, peeled, cut into thick matchsticks

1.25 litres water

3 teaspoon fish sauce

¼ teaspoon salt

¼ teaspoon sugar

To garnish

4 spring onions (shallots), rinsed, ends trimmed and chopped

lemon or lime wedges

cracked black pepper (parents)

2 bird's-eye chillies, sliced (parents)

1 Heat the oil in a large pot on medium heat, then add the onion and cook for 2 minutes or until soft.

2 Add the chicken to the pot and fry until slightly coloured.

3 Add the kohlrabi, water, fish sauce, salt and sugar to the pot and cook for 10–12 minutes or until the kohlrabi is tender, skimming any 'nasties' from the surface with a large spoon every few minutes.

4 Remove from the stove and spoon into bowls. Top with garnishes and serve.

Súp Nui Gà

CHICKEN, VEGETABLE AND MACARONI SOUP

Serves 2 adults and 4 littlies

Vietnamese mac and cheese, anyone? Except there's no cheese, but instead there's a hearty, healthy chicken soup with fun macaroni bits to fill you up. This dish is something I loved to eat when I was little. It's sort of a mix of Western and Vietnamese cuisine – my childhood version of pasta.

500 grams elbow pasta or macaroni

1 whole free-range chicken,
  cut into 4 pieces

1 litre chicken stock

1 litre water

2 brown onions, skin on and halved

2 carrots, unpeeled and cut into
  2-centimetre slices

2 corn cobs, cut into 4 pieces

1 small daikon, ends trimmed and cut
  into 2-centimetre cubes

1 teaspoon salt

3 teaspoons fish sauce

½ teaspoon sugar

To garnish

cracked black pepper

3 spring onions (shallots), rinsed,
  ends trimmed and chopped

4 sprigs coriander, ends trimmed
  and chopped

¼ cup fried shallots (optional)

For some more spice

extra fish sauce

1 bird's-eye chilli, chopped

lime wedges

1 Bring a large pot of water to a boil and cook the pasta until al dente as per the packet instructions, then strain and set aside.

2 Place the remaining soup ingredients in a large stock pot over a high heat and bring to a boil, then reduce the heat to medium and simmer for 20 minutes or until the juices coming from the chicken are clear. (You can remove a piece of chicken to test, then return it to the pot.)

3 Remove the chicken and onion from the broth. Discard the onion and set the chicken aside to cool.

4 Using a fork or your (clean) hands, shred the chicken and divide between serving bowls. Then add some pasta and broth, top with garnishes and enjoy!

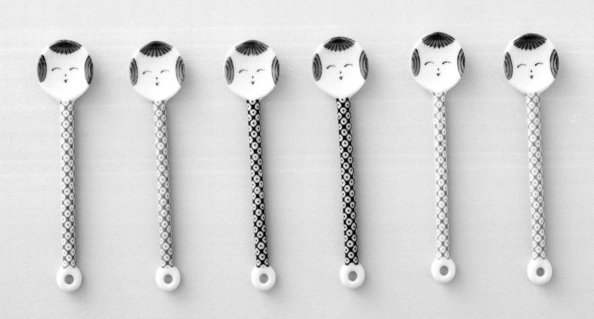

A FULL MEAL

Gỏi Cuốn

SUMMER RICE PAPER ROLLS

Makes 16 rolls

This is such a versatile dish – it can be made with anything leftover in the fridge – and the best part is that it's fresh, healthy and guilt free. This recipe is for the classic combo with pork belly and prawns, but it's only a starting point – you can mix and match it with whatever protein and veggies you have at home. I have a recipe for a sauce here (which my family loves to eat it with), but you could also use my nước mắm dressing.

1 kilogram pork belly, cut into 4-centimetre-thick strips

1 brown onion, halved

½ teaspoon salt

½ teaspoon sugar

1 teaspoon fish sauce

16 freshly cooked prawns, peeled and deveined

½ packet rice noodles, cooked per packet instructions

16 rice-paper wrappers

1 bunch garlic chives

1 bunch coriander, leaves picked

1 bunch mint, leaves picked

1 butter lettuce, washed and dried

For the original sauce

½ can black beans

4 tablespoons hoisin sauce

4 tablespoons tomato sauce

¼ teaspoon sugar

6 tablespoons water

½ teaspoon white vinegar

6 tablespoons roasted peanuts, finely crushed

Nước mắm dressing (alternative)

2 tablespoons fish sauce

2 tablespoons sugar

3 tablespoons warm water

1½ tablespoons lime juice or rice-wine vinegar

1 clove garlic, minced

1–2 bird's-eye chillies, minced (parents)

See over the page for the cooking steps.

1 Add the pork, onion, salt, sugar and fish sauce to a large pot and add enough water to cover 2 centimetres above the pork.

2 Place the pot over a high heat and bring to a boil, then reduce the heat to medium and cook, covered, for 30 minutes or until the juices run clear when you pierce the pork with a skewer.

3 Transfer the pork to a plate, cover with cling wrap and set aside to cool.

4 To make the original sauce, add the beans, hoisin sauce, tomato sauce, sugar, water, vinegar and half the peanuts to a small canister and blend with a stick blender, then add the remaining peanuts and stir to combine. (Or for the nước mắm, combine all the ingredients in a small bowl.)

5 Halve the prawns lengthways, leaving the tails intact, if you like. Flatten them so they have a 'butterfly' effect.

6 To assemble, place a large bowl of warm water on the bench. Dip a rice-paper wrapper into the water, then let the excess water drip off. Place on a plate. Add the ingredients one at a time starting with 2 prawn halves, then add some pork slices, followed by the rice noodles and then the herbs and lettuce. As you do this, stack the ingredients along the bottom third of the wrapper, leaving the edge clear.

7 Carefully roll the lower edge of the wrapper over the filling to make a log, then tuck in the sides and roll again to finish. Repeat with all the filling ingredients and wrappers. Enjoy with your chosen sauce!

Get the littlies
involved in rolling
their own!

Bò Kho

BEEF STEW

Serves 2 adults and 2 littlies

This is a Vietnamese classic – super comforting, super yum. Bò kho is a hearty beef stew with tender, fall-apart beef brisket cooked in a fragrant, spiced lemongrass broth. Serve it with either crispy Vietnamese baguettes or noodles and it's an absolute crowd pleaser. And if I were you, I'd double the recipe just so that you have leftovers to satisfy cravings for the next day! You will need to allow half an hour to marinate the beef, but after that, chuck it all in one pot and you're done. You will also need a strainer or muslin cloth.

1 kilogram beef brisket, cut into large cubes

1 teaspoon sugar

1 teaspoon salt

1 tablespoon five-spice powder

1 tablespoon vegetable oil, plus extra for frying

3 teaspoons fish sauce

1 stick cinnamon

1 black cardamom (optional)

3 pieces star anise

½ teaspoon cloves

1 teaspoon fennel seeds

2 brown onions, peeled and roughly chopped

5 cloves garlic, minced

2 tablespoons tomato paste

2 litres beef stock, plus 500 millilitres (optional if you are serving with noodles)

2 large stalks lemongrass, halved and sliced lengthwise

3–4 carrots, peeled and cut into 3-centimetre slices

4 tablespoons cornflour

6 tablespoons cold water

6 Vietnamese baguettes or 1 packet fresh egg noodles cooked per packet instructions, to serve

To garnish

Thai basil

garlic chives

Tommy's Tip

If you're serving the stew with noodles, you will need to add some extra beef stock to the stew to loosen it for a slurpable experience.

See over the page for the cooking steps.

1 Place the beef in a large bowl. To make the marinade, combine the sugar, salt, five spice, oil and 1 teaspoon of the fish sauce in a bowl and pour over the beef. Mix well to ensure all the beef is covered. Cover the beef and set aside in the fridge for at least 30 minutes (up to 5 hours if you have the time; the longer you leave it, the more flavoursome it becomes).

2 In a microwave-safe bowl, combine the cinnamon, cardamom, star anise, cloves and fennel. Microwave for 30 seconds, then transfer the mixture to a strainer or muslin cloth. Tie the muslin cloth to make a spice ball.

3 Add a little oil to a large pot over a medium heat. Add the onion and garlic and fry for 3–5 minutes or until soft.

4 Add the marinated beef to the pot and cook, searing the edges until the meat is browned all over.

5 Add the tomato paste, 2 litres stock, lemongrass and spice ball to the pot, then cover and cook on medium heat for 45 minutes.

6 Add the carrot to the pot, cover and cook for another 30 minutes or until the carrot and beef are tender.

7 Remove the lemongrass and spice ball and discard.

8 Mix the cornflour with the cold water and pour into the pot. Cook for 2 minutes or until the stock is thick, then season with the remaining teaspoon of fish sauce. If you are serving with noodles, add the extra 2 cups beef stock to the stew to loosen it.

9 Garnish with the basil and garlic chives and enjoy with some crusty Vietnamese baguettes or fresh egg noodles!

Cơm Gà Hội An

HOI AN CHICKEN RICE

Serves 2 adults and 2 littlies

This dish is essentially a Vietnamese version of Hainanese chicken rice. It requires a little bit of finesse – and you'll need to allow half an hour to marinate the chicken – but it's so worth it.

If you are using a rice cooker, be aware that all rice cookers are different, so use your judgement on how you usually cook rice. I usually use the Asian finger-line method (ha ha) but if you need a guide, 1 cup of rice to 1.5 cups of broth is the ratio for cooking on the stovetop.

1 whole free-range chicken

1 brown onion, halved

2 cups jasmine rice

Marinade

juice of 1 lime

2 tablespoons ground turmeric

2 teaspoons sugar

Salad

8 tablespoons hot water

4 tablespoons white vinegar

2 tablespoons sugar

1 brown onion, peeled and sliced

2 carrots, peeled and grated

½ daikon, peeled and grated

1 bunch Vietnamese mint
(or regular mint), finely chopped

Crispy garlic oil

4 tablespoons vegetable oil

12 cloves garlic, minced

Hội An chicken sauce

2 teaspoons oil

1 eschalot, finely chopped
(or ¼ brown onion)

4 tablespoons fish sauce

4 tablespoons white sugar

8 tablespoons water

2 tablespoons white vinegar

reserved fried garlic

See over the page
for the cooking steps.

1 Place the chicken in a large bowl. To make the marinade, combine the lime juice, turmeric and sugar in a bowl and pour over the chicken. Set aside for at least 30 minutes (1 hour if you have time).

2 To make the salad, put 8 tablespoons of the hot water, vinegar and sugar into a large bowl and stir until combined, then add the onion, carrot and daikon to the bowl and set aside until needed later.

3 To make the crispy garlic oil, add the oil and garlic to a pan over low–medium heat and cook for 3–4 minutes or until lightly golden, then pour the mixture into a bowl and set aside.

4 Place the marinated chicken and the onion in a large pot. Cover with water and then place a lid on the pot. Put the pot over a high heat and bring to a boil, then remove the lid. Reduce the heat to medium and simmer for 35 minutes.

5 Remove the chicken from the broth and set the broth aside to use later. Cover the chicken with cling wrap and set aside until cooled.

6 Using a fork or your (clean) hands, carefully remove the skin and set aside for later, and shred the chicken and set that aside too.

7 Add 3 tablespoons of the crispy garlic oil, 4 tablespoons of the turmeric chicken broth and the uncooked rice to a clean pan. Place the pan over a medium heat and fry, stirring constantly, for 4 minutes, then transfer the mixture to a rice cooker. Add 3 cups turmeric chicken broth and cook according to your rice cooker's instructions.

8 To make a sauce, add the oil and eschalot to a pan over a medium heat and cook until soft. Add the fish sauce, sugar and water and simmer for 3 minutes to slightly thicken the sauce. Remove the sauce from the pan, then add the vinegar and the reserved fried garlic mixture into the sauce.

9 Strain the onion, carrot and daikon pickle and place in a small bowl.

10 To serve, on each large serving plate arrange an upturned bowl of rice in the centre surrounded by chicken, chicken skin and salad. Pour some sauce over the top, mix it around and enjoy! Offer any remaining sauce on the side and garnish with mint.

Perfectly poached turmeric chicken rice, a fresh little side salad and a sweet sticky sauce to drench it all in.

YUM!

Lagu Gà

VIETNAMESE CHICKEN RAGU WITH PEAS AND POTATOES

Serves 2 adults and 2 littlies

This is a classic example of French-influenced Vietnamese food. Stewed chicken with mushrooms, peas and potatoes in a rich, flavourful tomato-based sauce – yummmmmm. Combine this with crunchy Vietnamese baguettes and you've got yourself a winner winner chicken dinner!

The dish usually uses a whole chicken broken down into bite-sized pieces, but I know how pressed parents are for time, so I've used chicken thigh fillets to make the dish a little easier to make. But feel free to break down a whole chicken and cut it into chunks for the traditional experience.

1½ tablespoons vegetable oil

3 washed potatoes, peeled and halved

4 free-range chicken thighs, cut into 4-centimetre pieces

1 brown onion, peeled and finely chopped

5 cloves garlic, minced

4 tablespoons tomato paste

2 carrots, peeled and chopped into 3-centimetre chunks

250 grams Swiss brown mushrooms, sliced

1 litre salt-reduced chicken stock

1 x 400 gram can diced tomatoes

6 Vietnamese baguettes or 3 serves garlic bread

1 cup frozen peas

1 teaspoon sugar

¼ teaspoon salt

2 teaspoons fish sauce

To garnish

4 spring onions (shallots), rinsed, ends trimmed and chopped

3 bird's-eye chillies, sliced (parents)

lemon wedges

1 Heat 2 teaspoons of the oil in a large pot over a medium–high heat and add the potato. Fry until sealed and golden, then remove the potato from the pot and set aside.

2 In the same pot, add 2 more teaspoons of the oil and the chicken pieces. Cook until the meat is lightly browned all over.

3 Add 2 more teaspoons of the oil and the onion. Cook until the onion is soft.

4 Add the garlic, reduce the heat to medium and cook until soft.

5 Add the tomato paste, stir to coat and cook for 2 minutes.

6 Add the potato, carrot, mushroom, stock and canned tomato and stir to combine. Bring to a boil, then reduce the heat to medium and simmer for 20 minutes or until the potato is cooked through.

7 Heat your oven and warm up the baguettes or garlic bread while you finish making the ragu.

8 Add the peas to the pot and bring it back to a boil, then reduce the heat and simmer for 2 minutes.

9 Add the sugar, salt and fish sauce, stirring to evenly distribute the seasoning, then turn off the heat.

10 Serve your ragu in bowls and top with spring onion and chilli, if using. Squeeze some lemon over the top and serve with bread on the side. Enjoy!

Tommy's Tip

My little hack for the extra oomph is to switch the baguettes for garlic bread – I know, controversial! But shh, don't tell my mum. The crispy edges combined with the garlicky soft bread is heaven!

NOODLES

Phở Gà Hà Nội

HANOI CHICKEN PHỞ

Serves 2 adults and 2 littlies + leftovers

Everyone knows of phở bò (beef phở) but not many people know of phở gà (chicken phở), which is a shame because: 1. It's just as tasty and, 2. It's so much easier to make! Phở gà has the same sweet, savoury, spiced broth filled with soft luxurious rice noodles as beef phở, but instead of being topped with beef it features perfectly poached chicken. Now I mean, c'mon, that sounds like a winner to me! The biggest game changer about phở gà is that I can get it done within 2 hours instead of the 5 hours needed to make phở bò (beef phở)! Don't get me wrong, I love beef pho but with less time and the same cravings for homemade phở, chicken phở has my back! Make this and eat it for dinner, then for breakfast or lunch the next day as leftovers and you'll start feeling like a real Vietnamese family! You will need a muslin cloth and a couple of big pots for this dish.

2 brown onions, halved

5–7-centimetre piece ginger, halved

2 sticks cinnamon

6 pieces star anise

1 tablespoon cloves

2 chicken frames (optional if using stock)

1.5 kilograms chicken necks
(optional if using stock)

1 whole free-range chicken

3.5 litres water

3–4 tablespoons fish sauce

2 teaspoons salt

40 grams rock sugar or 2 tablespoons
white sugar

1 bunch coriander, roughly chopped

2 bunches mint, roughly chopped

1 bunch spring onions, rinsed,
ends trimmed and sliced

1 kilogram fresh or 400 grams
dry pho noodles

To garnish

hoisin sauce

sriracha sauce

lime or lemon wedges

bird's-eye chilli, chopped

satê´ chilli oil (optional)

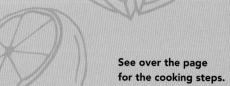

*See over the page
for the cooking steps.*

1 On a grill plate over a high heat, cook the onion and ginger, turning until both sides are charred. Set aside.

2 In a microwave-safe bowl, combine the cinnamon, star anise and cloves, and microwave for 1 minute.

3 Transfer the spices to a large pot and add the charred onion and ginger as well as the chicken frames, chicken necks and whole chicken. Add the water. Add 3 tablespoons of the fish sauce, the salt and the sugar, then place the pot over a high heat and bring to a boil. Reduce the heat to medium, cover and cook for 30 minutes, using a large, flat spoon to skim off any excess 'nasties' at regular intervals.

4 Remove the whole chicken and cover it with cling wrap. Pop it in the fridge to chill for 10 minutes.

5 Leave the stock on a medium heat (it should just be bubbling) for another 45 minutes.

6 While the chicken is cooling, mix the coriander, mint and spring onion in a bowl and set aside.

7 Remove the chicken from the fridge and use a fork or your (clean) hands to shred the meat.

8 If you are using fresh pho noodles, quickly (very quickly) blanch them in boiling water and then strain. If you have dried pho noodles, follow the instructions on the packet.

9 Line a large strainer with muslin cloth and place over a new pot. Carefully pour your pho into the pot; the liquid will drip through to the pot while the cloth will catch any bits you don't need. Your broth should be super flavoured by now – almost too flavoured, but that's okay because the noodles will lighten the flavour. Taste the broth and if it needs more saltiness, add the remaining tablespoon of fish sauce a teaspoon at a time.

10 To assemble, place some noodles in a large bowl, then add some shredded chicken, a handful of the mixed herbs and garnish with whatever condiments you'd like. Finish by pouring broth over everything, and enjoy that homey goodness.

FUN, FRESH FLAVOURS!

Garlic Prawn Hokkien Noodles

Serves 2 adults and 2 littlies

Thick, chewy egg noodles are so fun and easy to eat. Pair this with a yummy, finger-licking, garlicky sauce and you've got clean plates!

400 grams fresh hokkien noodles

1 tablespoon butter

1 teaspoon vegetable oil

4 cloves garlic, finely chopped

150 grams green beans, cut into 2-centimetre pieces

14 prawns, peeled and deveined

1½ teaspoons sesame oil

¼ teaspoon sugar

½ tablespoon soy sauce

3 tablespoons oyster sauce

½ teaspoon fish sauce

½ teaspoon white vinegar

3 tablespoons water

To garnish

4 spring onions (shallots), rinsed, ends trimmed and chopped

sriracha (parents)

chilli powder (parents)

lemon or lime wedges

1 Cook the noodles as per the packet instructions. Drain the noodles, then cool down by running cold water over them, and set aside to drain completely.

2 Add the butter and vegetable oil to a pan over a medium heat and leave until the butter just starts to bubble.

3 Add the garlic, green beans and prawns to the pan. Fry the prawns for 90 seconds on each side or until they just colour up, then remove the prawns and beans from the pan and set aside.

4 Add the sesame oil, sugar, soy sauce, oyster sauce, fish sauce, vinegar and water to the pan and cook on medium heat for 1–2 minutes or until the mixture just thickens.

5 Add the noodles to the pan, then mix and cook for 1 minute.

6 Turn off the heat, then return the prawns and green beans to the pan and mix thoroughly.

7 Place in serving bowls and top with spring onion and any other garnishes. Enjoy!

Japanese-style Pork, Tofu and Veggie Udon

Serves 2 adults and 2 littlies + leftovers

This dish is inspired by a Japanese classic: tonjiru. This is equally tasty with pork or without as a vegetarian dish. It's a hearty meal, so you can feed a big crew, or have leftovers.

1 teaspoon vegetable oil

1 brown onion, peeled and sliced

400 grams pork belly thinly sliced and cut into 3-centimetre pieces

½ small daikon, peeled, quartered lengthways and thinly sliced into triangles

2 carrots, peeled, halved lengthways and thinly sliced into halfmoons

2 spring onions (shallots), rinsed, ends trimmed and roughly chopped

3 litres dashi (this is a stock cube you mix with water to dissolve)

3 teaspoons soy sauce

2 teaspoons mirin

1 teaspoon sake (parents)

½ teaspoon salt

¼ teaspoon sugar

300 grams silken tofu, cut into eighths (double this if you are not adding pork)

600 grams udon, cooked according to the packet instructions

To garnish

2 spring onions (shallots), rinsed, ends trimmed and chopped

shichimi (parents)

extra soy sauce (parents)

1 Heat the oil in a large pot over a high heat. Add the onion and fry until just soft.

2 Add the pork belly and fry until lightly browned all over.

3 Add the daikon, carrot, spring onion and dashi. Bring to a boil, then reduce the heat to medium and cook, using a large, flat spoon to skim off any excess 'nasties' at regular intervals, for 12 minutes or until the daikon and carrot are soft.

4 Stir in the soy sauce, mirin, sake (if using), salt and sugar, then add the tofu and udon to the pot and bring back to a boil.

5 Serve in bowls and garnish with spring onion – if you want more of a kick, add some shichimi and more soy.

A ONE-POT WONDER!

Mì Xào Xì Dầu

STIR-FRIED NOODLES AND VEGGIES

Serves 2 adults and 2 littlies

This recipe can be as easy as finding whatever veggies and meat you have in your fridge or you can follow the ingredients list I have suggested. My mum still cooks this for me whenever she comes over, using whatever is lying around. This recipe includes a little family secret on how to get the perfect noodles for this dish – it's the microwave! Microwaving the fresh noodles before cooking them creates the perfect texture and really makes the dish what it is. Packets of fresh egg noodles can be found at Asian grocers and some supermarkets in the cold section.

350 grams fresh egg noodles

6 teaspoons vegetable oil

6 button mushrooms (approximately 200 grams), sliced

½ head broccoli, cut into small florets

½ capsicum, sliced into sticks

¼ onion, peeled and roughly sliced

3 cloves garlic, minced

300 grams beef rump or tenderloin, thinly sliced

3 teaspoons sesame oil

2 teaspoons oyster sauce

1½ tablespoons soy sauce

½ teaspoon sugar

½ teaspoon white vinegar

To garnish

3 spring onions (shallots), rinsed, ends trimmed and chopped

1 teaspoon soy sauce (parents)

1 bird's-eye chilli, chopped (parents)

1 Remove the noodles from the packet, then loosen them and layer them on a large plate.

2 Microwave the noodles for 90 seconds – they should feel a little dry.

3 Bring a pot of water to a boil and add the noodles, cooking for 1 minute.

4 Strain the noodles and rinse with cold water, then set aside to drain.

5 Place a large pan or wok over medium–high heat. Add 3 teaspoons of the vegetable oil, then carefully swirl the oil around to cover the bottom of the pan. Add the mushrooms and broccoli and cook for 4 minutes.

6 Add the capsicum and onion and cook for another 3 minutes, before removing the vegetables from the pan.

7 Add the remaining vegetable oil to the pan, swirling to evenly cover the base again. Add the garlic and cook until it just softens, then add the beef and fry until just browned on both sides.

8 Add the sesame oil, oyster sauce, soy sauce, sugar and vinegar and cook for 1 minute.

9 Add the noodles to the pan and toss to coat evenly with the sauce. Serve with your preferred garnish.

Creamy Miso Soba

Serves 2 adults and 2 littlies

This delish meal of creamy miso soba with chicken and mushroom has become a new Pham fam fav (say that fast three times, ha ha). This dish is so packed full of creamy umami goodness you can't go wrong. I'm salivating just describing it!

1 teaspoon vegetable oil

400 grams free-range chicken thighs, chopped

4 cloves garlic, sliced

200 grams Swiss brown mushrooms, sliced

1½ cups dashi (this is a stock cube you mix with water to dissolve)

8 tablespoons cream

1 tablespoon miso

1 teaspoon mirin

1½ teaspoons soy sauce

1 tablespoon butter

1 teaspoon sake (optional)

270 grams soba noodles, cooked 1 minute less than the packet instructions

To garnish

3–4 spring onions (shallots), rinsed, ends trimmed and chopped

2 packets roasted seaweed, roughly chopped

shichimi (parents)

1 Heat the oil in a pan over a medium heat. Add the chicken and fry until it is browned all over.

2 Add the garlic and cook until soft.

3 Add the mushroom and cook until just coloured.

4 Add the dashi, cream and miso and stir for 5–6 minutes until the mixture just thickens.

5 Add the mirin, soy sauce, butter and sake (if using) and stir well to combine.

6 Add the cooked soba noodles and mix thoroughly but gently to coat.

7 Transfer to serving bowls and garnish with spring onion and roasted seaweed – and some shichimi if you dare!

Tommy's Tip
I use soba noodles for this dish, but ramen or egg noodles work well too, especially if you're looking for a little bite from your noodles!

A FAVOURITE FOR KIDS!

Bún Gà Áp Chảo

LEMONGRASS AND SESAME OIL CHICKEN VERMICELLI BOWL

Serves 2 adults and 2 littlies

All-in-one healthy Vietnamese noodle bowls have become quite the trend recently and this recipe shows you how easy it is to make them at home. This dish is also a great way to level up your family's green intake. You can even turn it into a fun make-your-own-bowl night and get the kids involved.

1 packet rice vermicelli noodles, cooked as per instructions

1 bunch mint, roughly chopped

1 bunch coriander, roughly chopped

1 butter lettuce, roughly chopped

2 bird's-eye chillies, roughly chopped

For the lemongrass chicken

2 tablespoons oyster sauce

2 teaspoons sesame oil

2 teaspoons fish sauce

½ teaspoon sugar

4 tablespoons minced lemongrass (frozen minced lemongrass can also be bought from Asian grocers)

6 cloves garlic, minced

4 chicken thighs, skin on if possible

2 tablespoons vegetable oil

For the lemongrass chicken sauce

6 tablespoons water

2 tablespoons oyster sauce

2 teaspoons sesame oil

2 teaspoons fish sauce

½ teaspoon sugar

**For the pickled carrots
(optional but recommended)**

3 tablespoons rice-wine vinegar

3 tablespoons white vinegar

3 tablespoons hot water

3 tablespoons sugar

1 carrot, peeled and grated

For the nước mắm dressing

4 tablespoons fish sauce

4 tablespoons sugar

6 tablespoons warm water

2½ tablespoons lime juice or rice wine vinegar

2 cloves garlic, minced

1–2 bird's-eye chillies, minced (added after)

See over the page
for the cooking steps.

1 To make the lemongrass chicken, mix the oyster sauce, sesame oil, fish sauce, sugar, lemongrass and garlic in a large bowl. Add the chicken and mix it all well to ensure the chicken is coated, and allow to marinate for at least 15 minutes.

2 Add the oil to a pan over a medium–low heat. Add the chicken and fry, turning constantly to avoid burning, until cooked through. Transfer the chicken to a plate.

3 To make the lemongrass chicken sauce, add all the ingredients to the pan the chicken was cooked in. Stir to combine and cook over medium heat for 1 minute or just slightly thickened. Pour the sauce over the chicken and set aside.

4 To make the pickled carrot, combine the rice-wine vinegar, white vinegar, hot water and sugar in a bowl and mix until the sugar has dissolved. Add the carrot and set aside to pickle for at least 15 minutes before straining.

5 To make the nước mắm dressing, combine all the ingredients in a bowl and mix until the sugar has dissolved.

6 To serve, in each bowl place a serve of rice noodles and some mint, coriander, lettuce, pickled carrot and chicken. Garnish with chilli, a drizzle of the chicken sauce and a generous pour of the nước mắm dressing.

YUMMMM.

Easy Beef Phở

Serves 2 adults and 2 littlies

The belief that cooking phở takes hours is a myth. This quick-and-easy cheat's beef phở recipe will take you less than an hour so you have more time left for dishing out seconds to the fam.

1 stick cinnamon

6 cloves

3 pieces star anise

1 black cardamom (optional)

2 litres good-quality beef stock

1 teaspoon bone broth concentrate powder (optional)

2 onions, quartered

2-centimetre piece ginger, sliced

3 teaspoons fish sauce

3–4 teaspoons sugar

½ teaspoon salt

500 grams rump or tenderloin beef, finely sliced

1 kilogram fresh pho noodles or 400 grams dry pho noodles (cooked per packet instructions)

To garnish

1 bunch coriander, chopped

1 bunch spring onions (shallots), rinsed, ends trimmed and chopped

1 bunch basil, chopped

2–3 bird's-eye chillies (parents)

sriracha (parents)

hoisin (parents)

1 For the phở broth, place the spices (cinnamon, cloves, star anise and black cardamom) into the microwave for 1 minute. Remove from the microwave, place in a square of muslin cloth and tie up into a ball. If you don't have muslin cloth, use a clean, fresh Chux.

2 In a large pot, place the stock, bone broth powder (if using), onion, ginger, fish sauce, sugar, salt and spice ball, turn the heat to high and bring to a boil. Once boiling, turn the heat to low and simmer for 20 minutes.

3 Remove the onion, ginger and spice ball from the broth.

4 Place the beef in the stock and poach for 2–3 minutes, or until the beef is just cooked. Remove the beef from the broth and set aside.

5 In a separate pot, boil some water then add the fresh pho noodles for 1 minute and strain immediately.

6 To assemble, place the phở noodles, beef and herbs into bowls, pour over the broth and add any desired garnishes, then enjoy!

Bánh Canh Giò Heo

PORK TAPIOCA NOODLE SOUP

Serves 4 adults and 4 littlies

Growing up, we had this dish at least once a week and even now whenever I visit Mum there's a big chance that there'll be a steaming hot pot of bánh canh giò heo waiting for me. This is a great way to introduce the little ones to soup and noodles. The flavours are very simple and clean and it is loaded with bone-broth goodness. The noodles are thick and chewy, similar to Japanese udon but made from tapioca. It might seem daunting to give your kids big trotters to chew on but trust me, they love getting into it – and what kids don't love getting a bit messy at meal time?

1.5 kilograms pork hock or 1 kilogram pork ribs, cut into 2-centimetre pieces (your butcher can do this for you)

2 brown onions, halved

1 carrot, halved

1 small daikon, peeled and cut into 3-centimetre chunks

1 dried cuttlefish or 3 tablespoons dried shrimp

1-kilogram packet bánh canh tapioca noodles or udon noodles

1 teaspoon vegetable oil

250 grams bean sprouts

1½ teaspoons salt

1½ tablespoons fish sauce

½ teaspoon sugar

To garnish

½ bunch spring onions, rinsed, ends trimmed and chopped

1 packet fried shallots

½ bunch coriander, chopped

1 lime, cut into wedges

3 bird's-eye chillies, chopped (parents)

1 Bring 2 litres water to a boil in a large pot over a high heat. Add the pork hock or ribs, cover with a lid and bring back to a boil.

2 Strain the water from the pot. Rinse and strain the pork twice or until the water comes out clear and return to the pot.

3 Add 3 litres water to the pot and add the onion, carrot, daikon and cuttlefish. Bring the pot back to a boil, then reduce the heat to medium and simmer, with the lid half covering the pot, for 20–30 minutes or until the pork is tender.

4 Meanwhile, in a separate pot, bring 1.5 litres water to a boil over a high heat. Add the noodles and cook for 90 seconds.

5 Remove the noodles (keep the water in the pot) and place them in a strainer. Rinse with cold water, then add the vegetable oil and mix to prevent the noodles from sticking. Set aside.

6 When the pork is cooked, add the bean sprouts to the pot (it's easiest to dip them into the stock in a strainer) and cook for 1 minute. Strain the bean sprouts and set aside.

7 Season the pork broth with salt, fish sauce and sugar.

8 To assemble, add a serve of noodles to each bowl and top with a few pork slices. You can also add some of the carrot and daikon from the broth, if you like, and then garnish with a generous amount of spring onion and fried shallots, some coriander, a squeeze of lime and some chilli, if you like extra zing.

Tommy's Tip

An important step in this recipe is to clean and remove impurities from the pork by blanching it and rinsing it with water. This allows us to get a beautifully clear and clean broth flavour.

Mì Quảng

TURMERIC PORK AND PRAWN NOODLES

Serves 2 adults and 2 littlies

The combination of turmeric, coconut, prawn and pork in this recipe really makes this dish unique with a huge explosion of flavour. Not only does it taste amazing, it looks beautiful with the combination of lush green herbs and vibrant yellow from the turmeric. The coconut water gives the dish a slightly sweet hint (always a winner for kids) and the crunchy peanuts and fried shallots are a great way to introduce different textures. The traditional recipe doesn't have bok choy, but I'm always sneaking in some greens for the littlies!

For the marinade

½ red onion, peeled and finely chopped

2 teaspoons turmeric powder

2 teaspoons fish sauce

1 teaspoon sugar

6 cloves garlic, minced

2 teaspoons vegetable oil

500 grams pork belly, thinly sliced

10 large raw tiger prawns, peeled and deveined

2 bunches bok choy, washed and separated

300 grams dry mi quang noodles or dry pho or pad thai noodles

2½ teaspoons vegetable oil

500 millilitres coconut water

1 teaspoon fish sauce

¼ teaspoon sugar

¼ teaspoon salt

To garnish

4 sprigs mint, leaves finely chopped

4 spring onions (shallots), rinsed, ends trimmed and chopped

¼ cup fried shallots

3 tablespoons roasted peanuts, chopped

lime wedges

bird's-eye chilli, chopped (parents)

Tommy's Tip

You can find turmeric noodles from most Vietnamese grocers, but if you can't, then standard thick rice noodles will also work.

See over the page for the cooking steps.

1 To make the marinade, mix all the ingredients in a jug and set aside.

2 Place the pork belly in one bowl and the prawns into another. Give the marinade a good stir, then carefully pour half over the pork and half over the prawns. Mix thoroughly.

3 Cover the bowls with cling wrap and place in the fridge to marinate for at least 30 minutes.

4 Bring a pot of water to a boil, add the bok choy and cook for 90 seconds. Remove the bok choy from the boiling water and set aside.

5 Cook the noodles as per the packet instructions. Strain and rinse under cold water. Drizzle 1 teaspoon of the vegetable oil over the noodles and gently mix until evenly coated.

6 Heat the remaining 1½ teaspoons of the vegetable oil in a large pot on high heat, then add the pork and cook for 2 minutes.

7 Add the prawns and cook for another 2 minutes.

8 Add the coconut water and bring to a boil. Remove the prawns and set aside on a plate.

9 Cook the sauce on a medium simmer for 5 minutes to slightly reduce.

10 Add the fish sauce, sugar and salt to the sauce.

11 To serve, place a handful of noodles, a few prawns, a few spoonfuls of pork and sauce into a bowl. Top with garnishes and enjoy.

SNACKS

Paejeon

KOREAN VEGETABLE FRITTERS

Makes 4 large fritters

This is a Korean dish that has quickly become a household favourite. I mean, thin and crispy fritters dunked into umami dipping sauce – what's not to love? The best bit is, they're packed with so many veggies it's a great (and sneaky) way to get the little ones to eat (and love) vegetables! These are great as a lunchbox filler or on-the-go snack.

For the dipping sauce

2 tablespoons soy sauce

1 tablespoon rice vinegar

2 tablespoons water

1 clove garlic, minced

1 tablespoon honey

½ teaspoon sesame oil

For the fritters

1½ cups plain flour

4 tablespoons potato starch or cornflour

1½ teaspoons baking powder

½ teaspoon salt

3 cloves garlic, minced

1¼ cups cold water, plus more if required

½ carrot, thinly sliced into matchsticks

½ zucchini, thinly sliced into matchsticks

1 small potato, peeled and thinly sliced into matchsticks

5 spring onions (shallots), rinsed, ends trimmed and halved lengthways, then cut into 4-centimetre sticks

vegetable oil, for frying

1 To make the dipping sauce, combine the ingredients in a small bowl and mix thoroughly, then set aside while you make the fritters.

2 To make the fritters, mix the flour, potato starch, baking powder and salt in a bowl. Add the garlic and water, and stir until smooth. You want quite a thick batter, but if it needs loosening, add a little more water.

3 Mix the vegetables into the batter.

4 Heat 1 tablespoon of vegetable oil in a non-stick pan over a medium heat. Pour a cup of batter into the pan and cook for 4 minutes or until the bottom layer is golden, then use a spatula to carefully flip the fritter. Add 2 teaspoons of oil to the edges of the pan and cook for another 4 minutes.

5 Transfer the fritter to a plate lined with paper towel and repeat the process with the remaining vegetable batter. (You can keep the fritters warm in a low oven if you like, while you make the rest.)

6 Serve the fritters with the dipping sauce.

Patê Sô

VIETNAMESE FLAKY DUMPLINGS

Makes 20 dumplings

This is another dish that shows French influence. Its name literally translates as 'hot pie'. It's a flaky, crispy puff pastry filled with pork, cabbage and mushroom (yes, in my version I sneak in a couple of extra veggies). Pair this with a combination of tomato and sriracha sauce and you've got a winner.

1 teaspoon vegetable oil

½ small brown onion, peeled and chopped

4 Swiss brown mushrooms, finely chopped

1 cup finely shredded wombok (cabbage)

1 teaspoon sesame oil

1 teaspoon fish sauce

¼ teaspoon salt, plus extra

¼ teaspoon sugar, plus extra

250 grams pork mince

3 spring onions (shallots), rinsed, ends trimmed and finely chopped

1 large egg

1 tablespoon water

6 sheets frozen puff pastry, defrosted

To garnish

tomato sauce

sriracha (parents)

1 Put the oil into a large pan on high heat, then add the onion and mushroom and fry until soft. Add the cabbage and fry for a few minutes.

2 Add ½ teaspoon of the sesame oil and the fish sauce, salt and sugar into the pan and mix.

3 Remove from the heat, then pour the mixture into a large bowl and allow to cool.

4 Add the pork mince, spring onion, a pinch of salt, a pinch of sugar and the remaining ½ teaspoon sesame oil to the cooked vegetables and mix.

5 Whisk the egg and add the water in a small bowl to create an egg wash.

6 Use an 8-centimetre biscuit cutter or egg ring to cut 40 circles from the puff pastry. (You can also cut the puff pastry into squares.) Place 3 teaspoons of filling into the centre of each pastry circle.

7 Brush egg wash around the edge of each pastry. Place another circle of pastry over the filling.

8 Press the edges of the pastry with your fingers or a fork to make a seal.

9 Brush the egg wash over the top of each pastry and place on a tray. Repeat to make 20 pastries.

10 Preheat the oven to 180°C and bake for 15–20 minutes or until golden brown. If you're using an air fryer, cook the pastries for 8 minutes at 180°C.

11 Remove from the oven and allow to cool on the bench.

12 Enjoy as is or with tomato sauce and/or sriracha!

Chả Giò

VIETNAMESE SPRING ROLLS

Makes 50

Chả giò is one of those beloved Vietnamese dishes you order as soon as you see it on the menu. What's not to love about a crispy wrapping filled with a pork and prawn mixture that just oozes yum! The prep work – aka the rolling of the spring rolls – does take a bit of time, but if you get the whole family involved (which is usually what happens in Vietnamese families) you'll be done wrapping in no time! Chances are you'll have some leftovers to freeze for another day, so think about the long-term gains too!

1 packet frozen spring roll small wrappers (12.5 centimetres)

½ cup tightly packed shredded dried wood ear mushrooms

25 grams bean vermicelli noodles

300 grams pork mince

200 grams peeled and deveined prawns, finely chopped

1 carrot, peeled and grated

1 brown onion, peeled and finely chopped

½ cup water chestnuts, roughly chopped (optional)

½ teaspoon sugar

½ teaspoon salt

1 teaspoon chicken bouillon powder (optional)

2 teaspoons fish sauce

1 large egg

3 tablespoons water

1 tablespoon cornflour or plain flour

1 litre vegetable oil

Nước mắm dipping sauce

4 tablespoons fish sauce

4 tablespoons sugar

6 tablespoons warm water

2½ tablespoons lime juice or rice-wine vinegar

2 cloves garlic, minced

4 tablespoons roasted peanuts, finely crushed (optional)

1–2 bird's-eye chillies, minced (parents)

To garnish

1 butter lettuce, leaves washed and dried

1 bunch mint, leaves picked

1 bunch Vietnamese mint, leaves picked (optional)

Tommy's Tip
If you want the spring rolls to be extra crispy, you can use two wrappers.

See over the page for the cooking steps.

1 Remove the spring roll wrappers from the freezer and defrost on the kitchen bench.

2 Soak the wood ear mushroom and bean vermicelli noodles in a small bowl with enough warm water to cover. Leave for about 5 minutes.

3 Drain and roughly chop both, cutting the noodles about 4 centimetres long.

4 In a large bowl, mix the pork, prawn meat, mushroom, noodles, carrot, onion and water chestnuts.

5 Add the sugar, salt, chicken powder (if using), fish sauce and egg into the bowl and mix thoroughly.

6 In a small bowl, mix the water and cornflour until smooth.

7 Prepare a space for rolling your spring rolls – you'll need room for your wrappers, filling bowl, cornflour mixture and a tray for your finished rolls.

8 Remove the spring roll wrappers from the packaging and place on a plate.

9 Soak a paper towel in water and wring out most of the water. Use this to cover your wrappers. They tend to dry out quite quickly, so the moist paper towel helps prevent this.

10 Put a wrapper on a plate with a corner of the wrapper pointing towards you. Place approximately 1½ teaspoons of filling a third of the way from the corner of the wrapper (just a little below centre) and form a log with the filling.

11 Fold the bottom corner of the wrapper over the filling and upwards, then press tightly to remove any air.

12 Fold the left and right corners of the spring roll into the centre and again lightly press to remove any air pockets.

13 Tightly roll the spring roll up, until there is a triangle of wrapper left.

14 Dip your finger into the cornflour mixture and dab it onto the tip of the wrapper.

15 Roll the remaining part of the wrapper and gently press the tip to seal. Place the finished spring roll on the tray. Repeat until you run out of fillings or wrappers.

16 Heat up the vegetable oil in a large pot to 180°C (or until the oil bubbles when the end of a wooden chopstick is dipped into it). Then turn the heat down to a medium–high heat.

17 Fry small batches of spring rolls until golden – this should take 5–6 minutes. Make sure you don't overcrowd your pot as this will lower the temperature too quickly and you'll end up with sub-par crispness. Let the oil return to temperature before adding the next batch.

18 In a medium bowl, place the nước mắm ingredients and mix until the sugar has completely dissolved.

19 Serve as is with the dipping sauce or wrap with garnishes (lettuce, mint and Vietnamese mint) before dipping.

Get the kids involved with wrapping these yummy parcels!

Bắp Xào Bơ

BUTTER-SEARED CORN WITH DRIED SHRIMP

4 servings

This is something you can whip up in minutes, so it's perfect for taming those in-between-meal hungers! It's a relatively new street food in Vietnam that combines buttery sweet corn, umami dried shrimp and spring onion for that extra savoury taste. You can't get any better. This recipe uses canned corn to make it even easier. If you have time, you can use two cobs of corn instead and fry it until cooked before following the recipe!

1½ tablespoons dried shrimp (reduce to 2 teaspoons if you think your littlie won't like this taste)

2 tablespoons boiling water

½ teaspoon vegetable oil

1 can corn kernels, no salt, strained or the kernels from 2 corn cobs

2 tablespoons salted butter

½ teaspoon fish sauce

3–4 spring onions (shallots), rinsed, ends trimmed and chopped

To garnish

2 tablespoons fried shallots

sriracha (parents)

1 Place the dried shrimp a small bowl and cover with the boiling water to soften for at least 15 minutes, then drain.

2 Chop the dried shrimp finely, or you can use a food processor.

3 Heat the oil in a medium pan on a high heat until hot.

4 Add the corn kernels and dried shrimp and fry for 2–3 minutes or until lightly seared.

5 Add the butter and cook for 2–3 minutes until the butter has been absorbed by the corn.

6 Turn off the heat and add the fish sauce and spring onion and stir.

7 To serve, place a portion of corn into small bowls and garnish with fried shallots and sriracha (if using).

A great snack for hungry
little tummies!

Hoành Thánh

PORK AND VEGGIE WONTONS

Makes approximately 60

Hoành thánh is the Vietnamese equivalent of the Chinese wonton and this recipe is my family version. I like to add mushroom and carrot to give the wontons a little more vegetable substance. Hiding veggies is a controversial topic, but in my opinion, these wontons are tastier with the veggies. And let's face it, it always puts a smile on the face of parents when you get to sneak some extra veggies into the little one's diet! This recipe makes quite a big batch and I usually freeze the leftovers to use later for a meal when I'm short on time. These can be cooked two ways, boiled or deep fried. Boiled is the classic way, but who doesn't love a deep-fried dumpling?

60 wonton wrappers (these usually come in packets of 30)

1 litre vegetable oil (for deep frying, if that's how you choose to cook the wontons)

For the filling

400 grams pork mince

200 grams mushrooms, minced

2 carrots, grated

4 spring onions (shallots), rinsed, ends trimmed and finely chopped

4 cloves garlic, minced

4-centimetre piece ginger, grated

3 tablespoons soy sauce

1 tablespoon sesame oil

¼ teaspoon salt

For the dipping sauce

2 tablespoons soy sauce

3 tablespoons black vinegar

1 teaspoon sugar

1½ tablespoons water (to dilute the soy for kids)

1–3 tablespoons chilli oil (parents)

To garnish

3 spring onions (shallots), rinsed, ends trimmed and chopped

Tommy's Tip

I use Heng Shun Chinkiang black vinegar, which is available at most supermarkets. If you use a different brand you might get a stronger spiced flavour, so adjust the soy sauce and sugar to taste.

See over the page for the cooking steps.

1 To make the filling, mix all the ingredients in a large bowl.

2 Place the wonton wrappers on a board and put approximately 1½ teaspoons of filling in the middle of a wrapper. (You'll get an idea of how much filling you can add once you make a few.)

3 Brush water on the edges of the wrapper, then fold the wrapper over in half so you have a half-moon shape (if you're using round wrappers), or triangles (if using square wrappers), and press the air out of the wrappers, sealing the edges as you go.

4 Fold the corners of the wrappers back towards you to create the wonton shape, removing any air, and pinch to seal.

5 You can fry the original hoành thánh shape but I also like to make pyramid shapes for the fried ones – like in the pictures. You'll need square wrappers to make them in this shape. Add some filling as per step 2, then brush water on the edges of the wrapper and fold into a triangle. Take the two opposite ends of the triangle and bring them to the centre to form a pouch/pyramid, then press the air out of the wrappers, sealing the edges as you go.

6 Repeat for the remaining filling and wrappers.

7 Mix the ingredients for the dipping sauce in a small bowl.

For boiled hoành thánh

Boil water in a large pot. Using a slotted spoon, add dumplings into the pot for approximately 8 minutes (12 minutes for frozen). Be sure not to overcrowd the pot by adding too many dumplings at a time. Remove dumplings from the water and transfer to a plate. Garnish with spring onion and enjoy with sauce.

For fried hoành thánh

Line a plate with paper towel. Heat 1 litre vegetable oil in a large pot to 180°C or until a wooden chopstick bubbles when you dip it in. Carefully add dumplings (a few at a time) to the pot and cook until they are golden – 5–6 minutes. Remove the dumplings from the oil and drain on the paper towel. Let the oil return to 180°C before adding the next batch of wontons to ensure a crispy result. Enjoy with the dipping sauce.

Teach your kids how to use chopsticks – for eating and playing the drums at the dinner table.

Sinh Tố Bơ

AVOCADO SHAKE

Serves 1 adult and 2 littlies

When I was a kid, avocado shakes were one of my favourite treats. The first time I explained this to my non-Vietnamese friends they weren't convinced. 'What?' they said. 'Avocados are for savoury foods. No way can you have it sweet!' I always ended up changing their minds when they tasted an avocado shake!

2 avocados

2 tablespoons condensed milk plus
   1 tablespoon extra if you like it
   slightly sweeter

2 teaspoons sugar

¾ cup milk

2 cups ice

1 Place all the ingredients in a blender and blend until smooth.

2 Enjoy!

SWEETS

Creamy Mango Coconut Sago

Serves 6 adults

This is not a traditional Vietnamese dessert, but it's a new family favourite recipe I just had to include in this book. This is sure to satisfy a dessert craving, and it's perfect in summer when mango season is in full force. The slight tartness from the mango combined with the creamy coconut and the delicate texture of the sago is a crowd pleaser.

2 litres water

1 cup sago pearls

3 cups finely chopped mango (approximately 2 large mangoes)

¾ cup premium coconut milk

1 tablespoon coconut sugar or white sugar (optional and might depend on sweetness of the mangoes)

1 Bring the water to a boil in a large pot.

2 Add the sago, mixing thoroughly, then reduce the heat to medium–low and cook for 8 minutes, constantly stirring, until the sago is translucent.

3 Turn the heat off, cover the pot with a lid and let sit for 5 minutes.

4 Strain the sago pearls and run under cold water until cool, then set aside.

5 Combine 1½ cups of the chopped mango and ¼ cup coconut milk in a separate bowl and blend until smooth with a stick blender.

6 Stir the sago pearls into the mango mixture until well combined.

7 Combine the rest of the coconut milk and the sugar and mix until the sugar has dissolved.

8 To serve, layer a few spoonfuls of sago, a few spoonfuls of coconut milk and a few pieces diced mango into a glass. Repeat until the glass is filled, topping with any remaining mango – then enjoy!

Tommy's Tip

Some sago pearls are larger than others, depending on the brand. Larger will take longer to cook.

CREAMY!

Yum Cha Mango and Fruit Pancakes

Makes 8–10 pancakes

Everyone's favourite yum cha dessert is the famous mango pancake – silky, delicate, thin crepes filled with sweet, juicy mango and decadent whipped cream. Yes, even I'm drooling writing this. I always want my family to eat the food they love, hence this recipe is in this book! As long as you have a good non-stick pan you'll be making these in no time! Also, this recipe works with any soft fruit – strawberries, raspberries, kiwis, blueberries – the options are endless!

500 millilitres milk

2 tablespoons butter, melted

¼ teaspoon salt

1 teaspoon sugar

3 large eggs, beaten

1 cup plain flour

½ teaspoon vegetable oil

For the filling

300 millilitres thickened cream

1 teaspoon icing sugar (optional)

2–3 mangoes, peeled and cut into long strips or any fruit you'd like to use

Tommy's Tip

To give the cream a firmer texture (which makes it easier to roll), make sure the cream is as cold as possible before whipping. I sometimes add it to the freezer for 15–20 minutes before I start whipping!

And don't fret if you don't get the first crepe right – they are tricky even for the best of us! Just keep going and they'll eventually start to work. It just takes practice.

See over the page for the cooking steps.

1 Heat the milk in the microwave for 30 seconds or until warm to touch. (This helps prevent the butter from solidifying later.) Pour the milk into a large mixing bowl.

2 Add the melted butter, salt, sugar and eggs to the mixing bowl and whisk until evenly combined.

3 Sift the flour into the bowl and whisk until fairly smooth.

4 Pour the batter through a sieve into another large bowl to remove any lumps.

5 Heat the oil in a non-stick pan on medium heat until hot, then carefully spread the oil around the pan with a paper towel.

6 Turn the heat down to medium–low and pour in just enough batter to cover the bottom of the pan (about ⅓ cup in a 20-centimetre pan). Don't worry, the first pancake is always the chef's taster!

7 Swirl the batter in the pan until a thin layer evenly covers the bottom. Cook the pancake for 2–3 minutes or until cooked through and no longer sticky to touch. No need to flip it!

8 Gently remove the pancake from the pan and place on a plate to cool. Cover the pancake to prevent drying.

9 Repeat with the remaining batter.

10 Whisk the cream and icing sugar (if using) until soft peaks have formed. I use a hand beater but you can use a whisk if you want!

11 To assemble, place a pancake on a plate cooked-side down. Add a dollop of whipped cream across the centre of the pancake and place your fruit on top. Fold the bottom of the pancake over the filling, then fold in the sides and keep rolling to form a log.

12 Repeat until all the pancakes are complete.

13 Place the pancakes in the fridge for 20–30 minutes to firm up before serving.

Chè Trôi Nước

SWEET RICE DUMPLINGS

Serves 2 adults and 2 littlies

This is a picture-perfect dessert that you would be sure to come across in any street stall in Vietnam: cute little glutinous rice balls filled with a mung-bean paste, floating in a gingery sugar syrup – all topped with a generous spoonful of luscious coconut cream. Not only delicious, but also fun to make with the littlies. Get everyone together to help make this and enjoy as a family!

2 cups ice cubes

500 millilitres water

For the ginger syrup

110 grams roughly chopped palm sugar
  (approximately 1 cup)

2-centimetre piece ginger, peeled and cut
  into matchsticks

500 millilitres water

For the mung-bean filling

½ cup peeled dried split mung beans

1½ teaspoons sugar

For the dumplings

1½ cups glutinous rice flour

¼ teaspoon salt

200 millilitres water, boiled and then
  slightly cooled

2–4 tablespoons glutinous rice flour extra

To garnish

100 millilitres coconut cream

2 tablespoons toasted sesame seeds

Tommy's Tip

If you don't have time to stand and watch the sesame seeds in a frying pan so they don't burn, spread them over a microwave-safe plate and microwave for 2 minutes. Then mix up and microwave for a further minute – don't worry, they will still brown up nicely.

See over the page for the cooking steps.

1 To make the ginger syrup, add the ingredients to a small pot and bring to a boil over a medium–high heat.

2 Reduce the heat to low and simmer for 4 minutes. Remove the ginger from the syrup and reserve if you desire – I like to add it as an extra garnish later, but it's up to you. Set the syrup aside while you make the dumplings.

3 To make the filling, place the mung beans in a small pot and pour in just enough water to cover. Mix the mung beans with your hand, then strain and repeat this process until the water runs clear.

4 Add 1½ cups water to the pot with the cleaned and strained mung beans. Bring the pot to a boil over a medium–high heat, then turn the heat down to a low simmer. Simmer the beans for approximately 20 minutes or until soft and cooked through – make sure you stir the pot every 5 minutes.

5 Add the sugar to the mung beans and stir through.

6 Mash the mung beans with a potato masher until they turn into a paste. It should be a fairly dry paste that you can pick up and form into a ball. If the mung bean paste is too dry, add a little bit of water. If it is too wet, place it into a microwave and microwave at 1-minute intervals (uncovered) until the desired consistency.

7 Scoop 1 tablespoon of mung bean paste and roll it with your hands to form a ball. Repeat for the remaining mung bean paste – you should end up with around 10 balls.

8 Place the balls on a plate, cover with cling wrap and place in the fridge.

9 To make the dumplings, put the glutinous rice flour in a large mixing bowl and add the salt. Gently mix to combine.

10 Pour the slightly cooled boiled water into the bowl and stir to form a dough. The dough should be quite a watery, soft paste at this point.

11 Add 3 tablespoons of the extra glutinous rice flour to the dough and gently knead for 5 minutes. Your dough is ready if you can pinch some out and easily form a round disc out of it. If the dough is too dry and cracks when you try to make a disc, add 1 tablespoon of water at a time and knead until it reaches the right consistency. If the dough is too wet and won't form a disc, add 1 tablespoon of glutinous rice flour at a time and knead until the right consistency is reached.

12 Wet a paper towel and squeeze out the excess water to place on top of the dumplings as you make them so they don't dry out.

13 Remove the mung bean balls from the refrigerator and place on the bench.

14 Take 1–1½ tablespoons of the dough and form a ball, then with a rolling pin flatten the ball into a disc as thin as you can make it before it starts to fall apart (around 3 millimetres thick).

15 Place a mung bean ball in the centre of the disc and mould the dough around the mung bean until completely covered – you will have another ball, just now with the filling inside. The way I do it is to fold two sides together first around the mung bean filling, and then the other two sides together as this gives me a rough starting point. If you have any leftover dough, pinch it off and put it back with the other dough. If you have too little dough and there are gaps, you can patch it up with little pinches of dough.

16 Give the dumpling a final roll between your hands to smooth out the creases, then place the ball onto a large plate. Make sure you cover the plate with the damp paper towel to prevent drying out.

17 Repeat this process with the remaining mung bean balls. You will have more dumpling dough than you need, but don't worry – we use this in the next step!

18 With the remaining dough, take 1 teaspoon at a time and roll each into an approximately 15-millimetre ball.

19 Place a large pot of water over a high heat and bring to a boil. Place the mung bean dumplings and small balls into the pot of boiling water. Keep the heat on medium–high so the water is on a rolling boil.

20 Put the ice cubes and water into a large bowl. This is to cool the dumplings as they are cooked.

21 When a dumpling is cooked (3–5 minutes), it will float to the top – how cool is that!? Remove the cooked dumplings from the boiling water with a slotted spoon and place into the iced water. Repeat until all the dumplings are cooked.

22 Lift the dumplings from the iced water with a slotted spoon and transfer to the syrup.

23 To serve, place 2 large mung-bean-filled dumplings, a few small dumplings and a couple of tablespoons of ginger syrup into each small bowl. Drizzle with coconut cream and sprinkle with sesame seeds to finish.

Chuối Chiên

BANANA FRITTERS

Crispy on the outside, soft and sweet on the inside, banana fritters are always a crowd favourite. The Vietnamese version includes sesame seeds and shredded coconut in the batter, which makes a big difference to the crunch factor. Make these and you'll be surprised how fast they disappear.

6 overly ripe (but not squishy!) sugar bananas or lady finger bananas

½ cup plain flour

½ cup cornflour

½ cup rice flour

¼ cup sesame seeds

½ cup shredded coconut

¼ cup sugar

1 x 400 millilitre can coconut milk

⅓ cup cold water

2 litres vegetable oil for deep-frying

1 Cut the bananas in half lengthways and flatten out the curved side with a knife or spatula.

2 In a large bowl, add the flours, sesame seeds, shredded coconut, sugar, coconut milk and cold water. Mix until it forms into a batter.

3 Add the oil to a large pot and bring to a medium heat. Put a drop of batter into the oil and if it bubbles up, it's ready.

4 Add the bananas, a couple at a time, into the batter, making sure they are well covered.

5 One by one, carefully place a few battered bananas into the hot oil.

6 Fry the fritters until golden, flipping if needed.

7 Repeat for remaining bananas, allowing the oil to return to temperature each time.

Tommy's Tip

Use overly ripe monkey bananas (you know the small ones monkeys eat) or lady finger bananas. It won't taste good unless the bananas are almost black. Trust me.

Tommy's Tip

If you have time, throw the batter in the freezer for about 30 minutes to make it extra crispy.

CRUNCH!

Xôi Lá Dứa

PANDAN STICKY RICE

Serves 2 adults and 2 littlies

Nothing beats a fresh batch of steaming hot sticky rice. My recipe for this pandan sticky rice is kind of a cheat's version. Usually you'd have to blend pandan leaves and strain the water to use for soaking. The clean up is too much for me so I use the premade extract from a can and a little extra essence for the colour.

2 cups glutinous rice

1 can pandan leaf extract or ½ teaspoon pandan essence and 1½ cups water

¼ teaspoon pandan essence

1 can coconut cream

1 tablespoon sugar

To garnish

1 cup freshly shredded coconut (use frozen if fresh not available)

⅓ cup sesame seeds

6 tablespoons roasted peanuts, chopped

sprinkle of sugar (optional)

1 Fill a large bowl with the glutinous rice and enough water to cover it. Using your hands, wash the rice in a circular motion.

2 Strain off the starchy water and repeat until the water runs fairly clear (wash at least twice). Drain as much of the water from the rice as possible.

3 Pour the pandan leaf extract, pandan essence and half of the coconut cream into the rice and stir until evenly combined.

4 Cover and place in the refrigerator to soak for at least 5 hours (up to 12 hours).

5 Grab your steamer. I use a stainless-steel steamer at home but you can use a bamboo steamer if you prefer. If the holes are too large and you think the rice will fall through, line the steamer with some muslin cloth. (If you don't have any muslin, you can use a new, clean Chux.) Place the steamer over a pot of water, cover and bring to a boil. Add the sticky rice to the steamer and reduce the heat to medium.

6 Steam the sticky rice for 15 minutes. Stir with a spatula to evenly distribute the rice, trying your best to move the bottom layer of the sticky rice to the top. Then steam the rice for another 15 minutes. Finally, pour the rest of the coconut milk over the sticky rice and mix evenly. Steam for another 15–18 minutes or until the rice is cooked through.

7 Dust the sugar evenly over the sticky rice and gently mix through with a spatula.

8 To serve, scoop a portion of rice into each bowl and garnish with coconut flesh, sesame seeds, peanuts and sugar (if using).

Đậu Hũ Nước Đường Gừng

SOY PUDDING WITH GINGER SYRUP

Serves 6 adults

This silky, soft soy pudding with a sweet ginger syrup is so nostalgic to me as it was always my go-to dessert after a feast at yum cha with the family. This is a cheat's version of the classic as there's no need to soak the soy beans, cook them, blend them and strain them – ain't nobody got time for that. This is for when you and your family want soy pudding and want it now! This can be made with long-life soy milk from the supermarket, but I do recommend using the soy milk sold in Asian grocers (in the refrigerated section) for a more authentic taste.

1 litre soy milk

1 teaspoon agar agar

For the sugar syrup

1 cup roughly chopped palm sugar (approximately 110 grams) or ¾ cup brown sugar

2-centimetre piece ginger, peeled and cut into matchsticks

1 cup water

1 Pour the soy milk into a pot, then sprinkle the agar agar over the top and whisk to combine.

2 On a medium heat, bring the soy mixture to a boil, then turn down to medium–low and simmer for 2 minutes. You need to be very careful not to over boil and burn the mixture here as soy milk burns quite easily.

3 Remove the pot from the stove and strain the soy pudding into a large bowl, removing any bubbles from the surface.

4 Cool the pudding at room temperature for 10 minutes.

5 Cover the bowl with cling wrap and transfer to the fridge to chill and set for a minimum of 3 hours or until the soy pudding just holds together and is jiggly when you shake it.

6 For the ginger syrup, bring all the ingredients to a boil in a small pot. Simmer for 4 minutes to infuse the ginger flavour. Remove from the heat.

7 To serve, spoon a few large flat scoops of soy pudding into a bowl and top it off with ginger syrup.

Pandan Muffins

Makes 16 mini muffins or 6 large muffins

I always seem to have some overripe bananas at home. I don't know why, but I just never get to them on time! The fam absolutely loves when the bananas get overripe because it means I can make these sugar-free muffins. (I wouldn't put it past them to hide the bananas until they go overripe so I make these yummy treats, ha ha!) The pandan and coconut flavour are my little spin on Vietnamese sweet flavours and I think they go really well in the muffin. The pandan gives a fresh vanilla fragrance and the coconut makes them just that little bit more luxurious!

2 overripe bananas (the riper the better), mashed

½ cup milk

⅓ cup melted coconut oil

2 large eggs, beaten

½ teaspoon pandan essence

1½ cups plain flour

2 teaspoons baking powder

oil spray for greasing muffin tins or muffin patties

1 Preheat the oven to 180°C.

2 Whisk the banana, milk, coconut oil, eggs and pandan essence together in a large bowl.

3 In a separate large bowl, add the flour and baking powder and mix until even.

4 Make a well in the middle of the dry mixture and pour the liquid mixture into it.

5 Gently stir until just combined.

6 Spray your muffin tins with some oil or fill muffin tins with muffin patties.

7 Fill muffin tins about two-thirds full with batter and place in the oven to cook for 12–15 minutes for mini muffins or 20–25 minutes for large muffins. The muffins are done when they are golden and a skewer comes out clean.

8 Place the muffins on a bench to cool before enjoying.

HACKS

Microwave Pancake Mix Mug Cake

Makes 4 mug cakes

If you need to serve one hungry belly quickly, then give this recipe a try. It's an all in one, speedy and easy microwave mug pancake recipe that will be ready in no time.

1 packet pancake mix or use the recipe on page 142

8 tablespoons milk

1 tablespoon sugar

Optional fillings

chocolate chips

frozen berries

½ cup ricotta

Optional toppings

honey

maple syrup

1 Make the pancake mix as per the instructions or prepare the sheet pancake recipe.

2 Fill approximately ⅔ of a mug with the mixture.

3 Add 2 tablespoons of whichever optional fillings you desire. Gently stir until just combined.

4 Microwave for 90 seconds on high.

5 Repeat with the remaining batter.

6 Enjoy with maple syrup or honey.

Tommy's Tip

Different microwaves have different timings to cook a mug cake, so if you find that your mug cake isn't cooked all the way, microwave in 20 second bursts until it's just cooked.

Tuna Mayo Onigiri

Makes 4 onigiri triangles

These onigiri triangles are super quick to make and are perfect for road trips or when you are on the go! They also make use of leftover rice, which is always a win.

2 x 95 gram cans tuna in oil, drained

1 tablespoon kewpie mayonnaise

3 tablespoons furikake (optional)

1 cup water

1 teaspoon salt

2 cups leftover rice, warmed in the microwave

1 packet roasted seaweed sheets

1 Put the tuna and mayonnaise into a small bowl and mix until even.

2 Spoon the furikake, if using, onto a small plate and set aside.

3 Pour the water into a medium-sized bowl, then dip your hands into the water and make sure they're wet all over so the rice doesn't stick. Put ¼ teaspoon of the salt onto your hands and rub together to evenly disperse.

4 Grab approximately ½ cup of rice and form a disc, make a small indentation and fill with approximately 1½ tablespoons of the tuna mixture.

5 Wrap the edges of the rice disc around the tuna centre and gently roll to form a ball.

6 Shape the rice into a triangular onigiri shape, then roll the edges of the onigiri in the furikake, if using.

7 Repeat with the remaining rice and filling.

8 Stand each onigiri in the centre of a sheet of roasted seaweed on one of the edges of the triangle and fold the seaweed around so it wraps half the onigiri.

9 Eat straightaway or wrap in clingwrap for the perfect on-the-go snack!

Chicken and Corn Soup with BBQ Chicken

Serves 2 adults, 2 littlies + leftovers

This is the greatest hack I discovered for making chicken and corn soup – BBQ chicken from the supermarket! Instead of preparing a whole chicken, grab a chook bag and off you go. Having the chicken already cooked really saves time and then the rest is just pantry staples.

1 BBQ or roasted chicken

1.5 litres salt-reduced chicken stock

2 spring onions (shallots), rinsed

2 teaspoons soy sauce

¼ teaspoon salt

1 teaspoon fish sauce

2 teaspoons Chinese cooking wine (optional)

500 millilitres water

1 x 420 gram can creamed corn

6 tablespoons cornflour

2 large eggs, lightly beaten

2 teaspoons sesame oil

To garnish

cracked black pepper

sesame oil

3–4 spring onions (shallots), rinsed, stems removed and chopped

3–4 sprigs coriander, rinsed, stems removed and chopped

1 Remove and shred the meat from the roasted chicken. Reserve the bones for the soup.

2 Add the chicken bones, stock, spring onions, soy sauce, salt, fish sauce, cooking wine (if using) and water to a large pot and bring to a boil.

3 Simmer on medium for 8 minutes to extract flavour from the chicken bones.

4 Remove the chicken bones and spring onions from the pot, then add the creamed corn and shredded chicken.

5 Mix the cornflour with enough water in a small bowl until evenly combined.

6 Bring the pot back to a boil and slowly add the cornflour mixture while whisking.

7 Cook on a medium heat, stirring constantly, until the soup starts to thicken.

8 Bring the soup to a boil and turn off the heat.

9 Place a sieve over the pot and pour the beaten egg into the soup and mix thoroughly. This process allows the egg to drizzle into the soup and gives a lovely silky texture.

10 Add the sesame oil to the soup and stir until combined.

11 To serve, ladle some soup into each bowl and garnish as desired.

Tommy's Tip

To shred the chicken, place it in a bowl and use an electric mixer with a paddle attachment to shred.

French Toast Sticks

Makes 18 sticks

These French toast sticks are insanely addictive! There's just something about picking up sticks of French toast and dipping them into syrup that's just so fun to eat.

3 large eggs

½ cup milk

1 teaspoon vanilla extract

½ teaspoon cinnamon

½ teaspoon sugar

6 slices bread (I recommend thick brioche), each cut into 3 strips

butter (optional)

Optional toppings

icing sugar

maple syrup

honey

1 Preheat an air fryer or your oven to 180°C.

2 Place the eggs, milk, vanilla, cinnamon and sugar in a large bowl and whisk until well combined.

3 Dip the bread into the egg mixture and flip to coat on all sides, then place into the air fryer or oven on a tray.

4 Cook for 5–6 minutes on high in the air fryer or for 24 minutes in the oven (flipping in between). The sticks are ready when they are golden and slightly puffed.

5 Alternatively, you can cook these on a nonstick pan with a little butter, turning and cooking until evenly golden on all sides.

6 Dust with icing sugar and serve as is or with some syrup or honey on the side for dipping.

Easy Congee

Serves 2 adults, 2 littles + leftovers

If you grew up in a Vietnamese household, you would have been told that it is a sin to throw away rice. This is my way of making sure I never commit the ultimate sin as this recipe uses old rice to make a really quick and easy congee that tastes just like you've spent hours over the pot. My favourite part about eating congee is the endless toppings. You can totally change the flavour by changing the toppings and it's like you've made a completely different dish.

4 cups cooked rice

1.5 litres salt-reduced chicken stock

1 teaspoon fish sauce

½ teaspoon soy sauce

¼ teaspoon sugar

¼ teaspoon salt

To garnish

4 spring onions (shallots), rinsed, stems removed and chopped

4 sprigs coriander, stems removed and chopped

¼ cup fried shallots

4 poached or soft-boiled eggs (1 per serve)

splash of soy sauce

chilli oil (parents)

1 Place the rice and chicken stock in a pot over a high heat and bring to a boil, stirring to ensure the rice doesn't stick to the pot.

2 Remove from the heat and blend with a stick blender for 45 seconds or beat with a wooden spoon by hand for 4 minutes until the rice is roughly blended.

3 Return the rice mixture to a medium heat and simmer for 5–10 minutes or until the rice softens and the congee just thickens. The congee may thicken over time because the rice will continue to absorb moisture. You can always add more water or stock to loosen the congee to the desired consistency.

4 Season the congee with the fish sauce, soy sauce, sugar and salt.

5 To serve, place some congee into large bowls and garnish generously.

Flatbread Pizza

Yes, this one is definitely not Vietnamese, but it is a lifesaver when you need something quickly. It's one of my hack recipes as you can use basic pantry ingredients and whatever you have in the fridge! You can also use whatever flatbreads you can get your hands on. I like to use Lebanese flatbreads, but you can use anything you have around – maybe English muffins or even sliced bread. Also use whatever toppings you have in the fridge, such as sliced cheese, cherry tomatoes, onions, capsicum, olives, ham, pepperoni, fresh basil and even pineapple (if you're into that!).

4 flatbreads, English muffins or slices of bread

For the pizza sauce

1½ cups tomato passata

½ teaspoon sugar

¼ teaspoon salt

¼ teaspoon garlic powder

2 tablespoons extra-virgin olive oil

½ teaspoon dried basil

½ teaspoon dried oregano

Topping options

sliced cheese

sliced red onion

sun-dried tomatoes

olives

ham, diced

pepperoni

fresh basil

pineapple

1 Preheat the oven to 220°C.

2 Add all the pizza sauce ingredients to a bowl and mix until combined.

3 Spread the pizza sauce onto your base of choice and evenly cover the surface.

4 Add your preferred toppings.

5 Place the pizzas on a lined baking tray and cook in the oven for 8–10 minutes or until the toppings have cooked. If you have an air fryer, cook the pizzas for 4–6 minutes at 200°C.

So easy and quick!

Quick Fruit Ice Cream

Serves 3 adults and 3 littlies

Who doesn't love ice cream?! This recipe is for mango and coconut cream, but you can sub out the mango with any other frozen fruit and change the coconut cream for thickened cream. The ice cream tastes best right after you make it, but it can be frozen to be eaten later; however, just be warned it won't have that silky, smooth texture it does when you first blitz it. I love that this is a guilt-free treat that tastes just like real ice cream.

3 cups cubed frozen mango

1 cup coconut milk

1–3 tablespoons honey
(optional to add more)

1 Add all the ingredients to a food processor and blitz until smooth.

2 Enjoy immediately for a velvety gelato texture or freeze for 1 hour for a thicker ice cream texture.

Sheet Pancakes

Serves 2 adults and 2 littlies

The sheet pancake is just one of those hacks you wish you knew about earlier! No more slaving away on a single pancake at a time while hungry eyes watch the back of your head! If you haven't got the time to mix, prepare and wash your dishes (what parent does?), you can always use a box of pancake mix (don't worry I do this too!).

1 tablespoon melted butter or vegetable oil

For the pancake batter

1 cup milk, plus ¼ cup more to loosen (room temperature or slightly warmed in a microwave)

2½ tablespoons butter, melted

1 large egg, beaten

1 teaspoon vanilla extract (optional)

1½ cups plain flour

2 teaspoons sugar

3 teaspoons baking powder

Optional fillings

frozen berries

chocolate chips

Quick microwave fruit compote (optional)

½ cup frozen berries of choice

⅓ cup water

½ cup white sugar

Optional toppings

maple syrup

golden syrup

whipped cream

1 Preheat the oven to 220°C.

2 To make the batter, whisk the milk, butter, egg and vanilla (if using) together in a large bowl.

3 Add the flour, sugar and baking powder into another large bowl and mix until even. If the batter is too thick, loosen it with the extra milk – it needs to be easy to pour.

4 Make a well in the middle of the dry mixture and pour the liquid mixture into the centre. Gently stir until just combined.

5 Place a sheet of baking paper on a large, shallow baking tray. Lightly brush the baking paper with melted butter or oil.

6 Sprinkle optional fillings on top of the baking paper sheet, if using.

7 Pour the batter evenly over the baking tray and smooth it out with a spatula. Place it in the oven and cook for 5–7 minutes or until golden.

8 To make the fruit compote, add the ingredients into a large microwave-safe bowl and mix until even. Microwave for 4 minutes, then stir to even out the sauce and microwave for another 3 minutes.

9 To serve, cut the pancake sheet into triangles/squares/ whatever shape your child is in the mood for and stack onto plates, serving with fruit compote (if using) and any additional toppings.

spaghetti Game

This little game here is a great way to get the little ones to work on their fine motor skills and concentration! There's also an extra bonus game, so two games in one – woo-hoo!

What you will need

Metal or plastic strainer

Dry spaghetti

A small toy

1 Place the strainer on the table or floor, with the large opening facing up.

2 Encourage your littlie to thread a piece of spaghetti through a hole from the outside of the strainer and across the middle to a hole on the other side. Place as many pieces of spaghetti through the holes as you can, creating a sort of nest or platform in the middle of the strainer.

3 To advance this play, place a toy on top of the spaghetti, then slowly pull out each piece of spaghetti until the toy falls through.

Tommy's Tip
This activity is great for practising fine motor skills.

Frozen Rescue

I've never met a kid who doesn't love playing with water especially when they shouldn't be (ha)! This is a good way to let the little ones explore and use that urge to play with water in a fun and new way!

What you will need

Small toys or flowers

Plastic containers

Water

Freezer

1 Place 1 or 2 small toys or trinkets or flowers/plants into each plastic container.

2 Cover with water and place in the freezer until frozen.

3 Remove the frozen ice blocks from the containers, then take outside with a jug of warm water (not too hot!).

4 Allow your littlie to rescue the toys by pouring the water over the ice. They can also use a plastic hammer or other tool to break the ice.

Extra activity

Instead of using ice, you can make lava-like jelly to capture your toys. Place water and agar agar into a large pot, bring to the boil, then add desired food colouring. Pour mixture into the large tupperware container and add desired toys and place in the refrigerator. Once set, allow kids to play with their toys stuck in lava – kids will love crushing and squeezing the jelly!

Tommy's Tip

Great summer activity that involves water play.

Guessing Game

This activity is great for getting the little ones to think about the shapes of objects and toys. And they love a surprise!

What you will need

Toys like shapes or letters

Foil

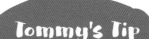

Tommy's Tip

Instead of using toys, you can wrap up different (safe) kitchen utensils for them to guess. It's a great way for them to learn about the kitchen too!

1 Wrap toys in foil.

2 Place them in a large bucket or on a tray.

3 Get the little ones to describe the object, for example: it's round, flat, spiky, rough, has holes.

4 Guess what the object is.

5 Unwrap and repeat.

Make Your Own Shaker Instrument

Get creative and make maracas with everyday kitchen items! Make sure to secure the items tightly though if your little one tends to put things in their mouth.

What you will need

Clear plastic cups/old spice shaker bottles

Pasta/rice/anything that will fit inside the bottles

1 Fill old spice bottles and/or plastic cups with pasta, rice or fried beans.

2 Seal the bottles or cups, taping them tightly and securely.

3 Have a dance party with your new maracas!

Threading Game

Practise patience and fine motor skills in this fun threading game.

What you will need

Dry spaghetti, chopsticks or skewers

Egg carton, a lump of playdough or empty box

Cheerios, macaroni or pasta shapes that the stick you are using will fit through

1 Push sticks of spaghetti, chopsticks or skewers (or whatever you are using as the stick) into a holder such as an egg carton, playdough or empty box.

2 Thread the macaroni or other item you're using as the stacking item, and create a fun tower.

Tommy's Tip
Level it up with a race to see who can stack the items the fastest!

Sorting Colours

An awesome activity for sorting shapes and colours, as well as making patterns and pictures!

What you will need

Shaped pasta (such as penne) or rice

White vinegar

Food colouring (different colours)

Ziplock bags

1 Add a handful of shaped pasta or rice, 1 teaspoon vinegar and 1 teaspoon food colouring to a ziplock bag.

2 Close the bag tightly and shake until the pasta or rice is evenly covered.

3 Place the pasta or rice onto a plate to dry.

4 Repeat using a different colour this time.

5 Once dried, mix the colours and allow the children to sort and also encourage them to use the pasta or rice to create a picture.

Make Your Own Noodles

The process of making noodles is such a fun way to get kids in the kitchen. Rolling, kneading, cutting and dusting are all really fun things to do with food!

What you will need

3 cups plain flour, plus extra

¾ cup warm water

½ teaspoon salt

1 teaspoon white sugar

Food colouring (if desired)

1 Place all the ingredients in a large mixing bowl, including the food dye, if using.

2 Mix and knead until smooth – please note that if you have used colouring, it will stain little hands!

3 Cover and set aside for 30–60 minutes.

4 Take out, divide the dough into four and dust with extra flour.

5 Roll with a rolling pin as flat as possible.

6 Dust with more flour and then fold/roll the sheet and cut into noodles!

7 To cook, bring a pot of water to a boil. Add the noodles and cook for approximately 3 minutes or until al dente and enjoy with sauce of choice!

Magic Rocks

We all love a bit of magic! These fun magic rocks are great for the little ones to explore different ways of getting their small toys out of the magic rocks! For extra fun, give them some vinegar in a spray bottle and let the fizzing begin.

What you will need

⅓ cup bicarbonate of soda

1 tablespoon white vinegar

Food colouring

Toy to place inside (per rock)

Tommy's Tip
You can also use ice-cube trays (shaped ones are great) as a mould for your magic rocks!

1 Place all the ingredients except the toy in a large bowl and mix until well combined. It should form a very thick paste, so add more vinegar if too dry or more bicarb if too wet.

2 Handling the mixture may stain little hands, so use plastic gloves if desired. Place 2 tablespoons of the mixture in your hand and create a sort of half-moon. Repeat so you have two half-moons.

3 Place a small toy in the centre of one of the halves and squeeze the other half against it to create a full ball.

4 Place the magic rock on a plate and put in the sun to dry.

5 Kids can either crack the magic rocks with tools to reveal the toy inside or they can place the rocks in a bowl of vinegar and watch it fizz!!

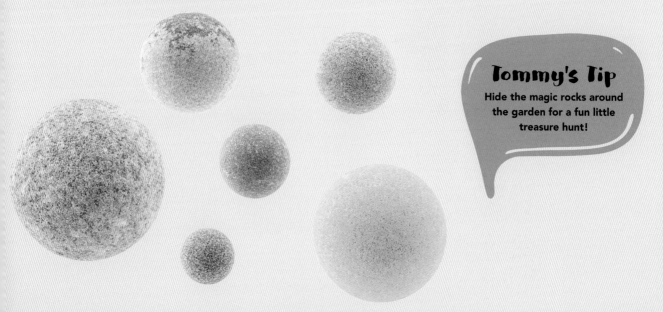

Tommy's Tip
Hide the magic rocks around the garden for a fun little treasure hunt!

Arts and craft

Using old paper plates, bowls and disposable cutlery is a great way to reuse and recycle. Kids love a good craft session and this is just a fun way to get them using their imagination!

What you will need

Disposable utensils, disposable plates and bowls

Glue

Colouring pencils or textas

Imagination

Tommy's Tip

For this craft activity you can use anything you have around the house as well – cardboard packaging, cartons, plastic lids and so on.

INDEX

ACKNOWLEDGEMENTS

To my mum, thank you for introducing me to all the wild flavours of Vietnamese food when I was young and for passing on your passion for cooking. But most importantly, thank you for showing me that cooking for your family is one of the greatest acts of love. I love you, Me.

To my mother-in-law, thank you for guiding me through many of the recipes that have made it into this book and for always being a call away when I need to ask which one is winter melon and which one is hairy melon for the hundredth time.

To Miles, my little foodie, who has taught me the importance of family and preserving our heritage. You're the perfect person to help me navigate writing this book.

To my amazing partner, Wendy – the love of my life. Without you I would have nothing. Thank you for driving me to push myself to be a better person. Thank you for taking on the tremendous responsibility of being the rock of our family, while I chased my dreams. You've sacrificed more than you should have and I will forever be grateful for your love.

Thanks also to Sharon Finnigan of SF Management, Andrew Young and Lantern Studios, Annette Forrest, Dixie Elliot and Sarah Jane Hallett. And to Melissa Leong. And at Penguin Random House: Jess Owen, Claire de Medici and Becca King.

PENGUIN BOOKS

UK | USA | Canada | Ireland | Australia
India | New Zealand | South Africa | China

Penguin
Random House
Australia

Penguin Random House Australia is part of the Penguin Random House group of companies whose addresses can be found at global.penguinrandomhouse.com.

First published by Penguin Books, an imprint of Penguin Random House Australia Pty Ltd, in 2023

Printed in China

Penguin Random House Australia uses papers that are natural and recyclable products, made from wood grown in sustainable forests. The logging and manufacture processes are expected to conform to the environmental regulations of the country of origin.

A catalogue record for this book is available from the National Library of Australia

ISBN 978 1 76 134088 8 (Paperback)

penguin.com.au

We at Penguin Random House Australia acknowledge that Aboriginal and Torres Strait Islander peoples are the Traditional Custodians and the first storytellers of the lands on which we live and work. We honour Aboriginal and Torres Strait Islander peoples' continuous connection to Country, waters, skies and communities. We celebrate Aboriginal and Torres Strait Islander stories, traditions and living cultures; and we pay our respects to Elders past and present.